Contents

CONTENTS

Introduction: Collection Assessment in Music Libraries

Jane Gottlieb

Assessment of a library collection is an essential component of the collection development process. In music libraries, discussion of evaluation processes is complicated by the fact that collections consist of materials in different physical formats. The standard tools of evaluation or assessment must be carefully adapted for the study of music collections. The Research Libraries Group (RLG) led the effort in creating a national project for collection evaluation with the development of the RLG Conspectus in the late 1970s. The Conspectus format began to be adapted by regional library consortiums in the early 1980s. Through regional assessment projects, music librarians in all types of libraries have the opportunity to undertake assessment of their collections as part of a coordinated plan. The papers presented in this publication—originally presented at a plenary session at the 1991 Music Library Association annual meeting—contain an overview of the current approaches towards and concerns about collection assessment for music libraries in the 1990s. By understanding and utilizing the methodologies available to evaluate their collections, music librarians will better insure that they are fulfilling their missions to meet their users' needs.

Assessment or evaluation of a library collection is an essential component of the collection development process. Library collections are developed to meet the needs of a particular clientele, and the librarians responsible for overseeing these collections must periodically assess, evaluate, and appraise holdings to insure that their collections meet the needs of their users.

These relatively simple concepts often become clouded by the confusion and complexity surrounding discussion of library

Jane Gottlieb is Head Librarian, The Juilliard School, New York, New York. She is responsible for collection development and evaluation of the library's collection of music, dance, and drama materials. She was a member of METRO's Music Task Force to design Supplemental Guidelines for evaluating music collections.

collection evaluation (or assessment) methods. In music libraries, discussion of evaluation processes is further complicated by the fact that collections consist of materials in different physical formats (scores, books, periodicals, sound recordings, films and videos, and archival materials) which are subjected to a variety of cataloging and classification practices. The standard tools of evaluation or assessment must be carefully adapted for the study of music collections.

Interest in utilizing systematic methods of collection evaluation developed in the library community in the mid-1970s, with the awareness that the budget of any individual library would never be able to support the purchase of all available literature in a particular discipline. At the same time, the existence of national bibliographic databases and consortia allowed possibilities for determining what materials were held by other libraries, and coordinating collection development responsibilities among institutions.

The Research Libraries Group (RLG) led the effort in creating a national project for collection evaluation with the development of the RLG Conspectus in the late 1970s; the Music Program Committee of RLG worked within this framework to create the RLG Music Conspectus in the early 1980s. In 1986, the Music Library Association (MLA) Subcommittee on Collection Assessment (Resource Sharing and Collection Development Committee) proposed the creation of a database to describe a "National Music Collection." Whereas participation in the RLG Conspectus project was limited to large research libraries, the proposed National Music Collection database would consist of information from libraries of all sizes and types.[1]

This particular project never came to pass, and with the dissolution of RLG's Music Program Committee in 1989, interest in the Conspectus project within MLA appeared to wane. Librarians in non-research libraries were typically not as likely to participate in collection evaluation projects, assuming that the only method available was the Conspectus approach.

The Conspectus format began to be adapted by regional library consortia in the early 1980s. These groups saw systematic collection evaluation as a useful tool for developing resources regionally. Through these regional assessment projects, music librarians in all types of libraries had the opportunity to undertake assessment of their collections as part of a coordinated plan.

Perhaps because the RLG Conspectus and its off-shoots are the most visible tools of systematic collection assessment, librarians are often unaware of collection assessment methodologies other than the Conspectus approach. The Conspectus is, in fact, merely a format for recording assessment information; the information itself can be compiled using a variety of methods. Further, because the most visible tools of collection assessment have been developed nationally or regionally, and the pressure to participate in these projects often comes from outside the library, librarians can too easily forget about the direct relationship between collection development and collection evaluation, as well as the potential benefits of collection evaluation for library users.

An American Library Association (ALA) publication—*Guide to the Evaluation of Library Collections*[2]—contains a comprehensive overview of the various methods of collection-assessment, including an itemization of the advantages and disadvantages of each. These methods include:[3]

1. checking lists, bibliographies, catalogs and other sources against the library catalog;
2. direct examination of the collection (or shelf-scanning);
3. compilation of comparative statistics (including size of collection, shelflist measurement, growth rate, expenditures, and collection overlap);

4. application of collection standards prepared by accrediting organizations or other professional associations;
5. circulation studies;
6. survey of user opinions;
7. shelf-availability studies;
8. analysis of interlibrary-loan statistics; and,
9. citation studies.

None of these methods is considered to be ideal, and most libraries benefit from using several methods of collection assessment in combination.

The papers presented here are about various aspects of the subject of collection assessment in music libraries. They were originally presented at a plenary session chaired by John Roberts (Music Librarian, University of California at Berkeley) and sponsored by the Resource Sharing and Collection Development Committee at the 1991 Music Library Association annual meeting in Indianapolis, Indiana. As a whole, these papers contain descriptions of current approaches toward and concerns about collection assessment for music libraries.

Peggy Daub describes the RLG Music Conspectus and its advantages and disadvantages as an assessment tool. The assignment of an ALA numerical code to represent "Current Collecting Level" for a Conspectus line can be done by using various assessment methodologies: list checking, shelflist measurement, shelf-scanning, etc. However, the RLG Conspectus format, with its ties to the Library of Congress *Classification* schedule, proves to be a problematic tool for evaluating collections of sound recordings, which typically are not classified in music libraries.

Elizabeth Davis describes the development of "Supplemental Guidelines" for evaluating music collections as part of a regional plan. The METRO Collection Inventory Project is modeled on the

RLG Conspectus. The "Supplemental Guidelines" recommend various published bibliographies as benchmarks, or sources that can be checked against the library catalog to establish collecting levels. The obvious advantage of list-checking as an assessment methodology is that it helps to identify lacunae in the collection. In recommending benchmark sources and establishing their collection levels, the METRO Music Project Task Force dealt with each format (scores, books, periodicals, and sound recordings) separately.

Sherry Vellucci examines the OCLC Online Computer Library Center, Inc./AMIGOS product for automated collection evaluation. The basic assessment principle of the compact-disc product is, again, list-checking (the individual library's catalog against parts of the OCLC database), in this case with all the advantages (and disadvantages) of automation. Vellucci evaluates the AMIGOS product as a tool for music libraries.

Finally, Lenore Coral offers a candid and focused critique of the Conspectus approach to collection assessment. She reminds us of the need to question the basic purpose behind any assessment endeavor: is it to compare the collections held by different institutions (a commonly assumed usage of the RLG Conspectus), or to determine whether an institution's collection is meeting the needs of its clientele?

It is hoped that these papers will help to inform librarians about the possibilities and techniques of collection assessment for music libraries in the present decade. In the process, some questions will be answered and others posed that are left unanswered. Library collections will continue to grow in size and scope, the tools to manage them will continue to expand in complexity, and user populations will inevitably change. By understanding and utilizing the methodologies available to evaluate their collections, librarians will better insure that they are fulfilling their mission to meet their users' needs.

References

1. Joan D. Kunselman, Peggy Daub, and Marion Taylor. "Toward Describing and Assessing the National Music Collection." *Notes* 43 (Sept. 1986):7–13.

2. Barbara Lockett, ed. *Guide to the Evaluation of Library Collections.* Chicago: American Library Assn., 1989.

3. Lockett, *Guide*, iii–iv.

THE RLG MUSIC CONSPECTUS:
ITS HISTORY & APPLICATIONS

Peggy Daub

ABSTRACT: The Research Libraries Group (RLG) Music Conspectus consists of 161 segments, or "lines," which together attempt to provide description of the universe of library holdings of music materials. Each line represents a Library of Congress *Classification (LCC)* class number. Bibliographers assign two codes to represent existing collection strength and current collecting intensity. In an effort to verify and compare numerical values assigned to music research collections, the RLG Music Program Committee embarked upon a shelflist count in the early 1980s. They also worked to use the Conspectus to describe sound recording collections, which are typically not organized according to the *LCC*. Applications and use of the Conspectus in music libraries are surveyed and assessed.

Much has been said and written about the Conspectus, including the following:

"The Conspectus is an overview, or summary, arranged by subject, of existing collection strengths and future collecting intensities."[1]

"The Conspectus is the matrix of collection depth indicators for all of the participating libraries."[2]

"The Conspectus permits institutions to communicate information about collections in common terms and to make local decisions in light of other members' holdings."[3]

"The Conspectus gives us a common language in which to describe our holdings."[4]

Peggy Daub is Head of Special Collections and Arts Libraries at the University of Michigan in Ann Arbor. She was responsible for collection development as Head of the Music Library at the University of Michigan from 1982 to 1989, and served on the Music Library Association's Subcommittee on Collection Assessment, Resource Sharing and Collection Development Committee. She was Chair of the Research Libraries Group Music Program Committee from 1985 to 1987.

> "[The Conspectus] is useful, although we are not clear about the exact
> nature of its usefulness. Its importance lies in its effectiveness in sup-
> porting scholarship."[5]

"The Conspectus" is one of those phrases that we've all heard ban-
died about. It has, indeed, entered the lexicon of library jargon. The
present paper serves mainly to describe how the music portion of
the Conspectus came to be, and to examine how it has been used
and accepted.

DEFINITION

The Music Conspectus as it currently stands consists of 161
segments, or "lines", which together attempt to provide a description of the universe of library holdings of music materials—mainly
music books, scores, and sound recordings. The bulk of the Music
Conspectus (139 of the 161 lines) covers music books, periodicals,
and scores, and has been defined by breaking up the Library of
Congress *Classification* (LCC) classes M, ML, and MT. For example,
definitions for lines 58–74 of the Music Conspectus, which corre-
spond to LCC classes ML1 to ML109, are shown in table 1.

For each line of the Conspectus a subject specialist assigns
two values to represent the collection. One value is for existing collection strength (ECS), and the other is for current collecting intensity (CCI). The ECS shows how strong that portion of the collection
is at present (a snapshot, so to speak) and the CCI indicates an in-
tention to continue building it. The ECS and CCI are expressed in
numbers from 0 to 5, using the definitions shown in table 2. The
letter codes may be added to help define the ECS or CCI further by
indicating the span of languages collected (or, for sound recordings,
the span of record labels collected). Finally, explanatory notes (in
free form, using any wording) may be attached to the Conspectus
line giving more details of local holdings in that area. These prose

Table 1: Definitions For Lines 58–74 Of The Music Conspectus

ID	LC CLASS	SUBJECT
MUS58	ML1	Periodicals—United States
MUS59	ML4	Periodicals—Before 1800
MUS60	ML5	Periodicals—After 1800-Foreign
MUS61	ML12–21	Directories
MUS62	ML25–28	Publications of Societies
MUS63	ML29–31	Music Foundations
MUS64	M32–38	Publications of Institutions and Festivals
MUS65	ML40–46	Programs and Advertisements. Scrapbooks
MUS66	ML47–54	Librettos
MUS67	ML55–60	Collected Literary Works (Essays, etc.)
MUS68	ML62–85	Special Topics
MUS69	ML86–89	Musical Iconography
MUS70	ML90	Writings of Musicians
MUS71	ML93–96	Musical Paleography
MUS72	ML96.4–96.5	Facsimiles
MUS73	ML97	Catalogs of Collectors, Dealers, etc.
MUS74	ML100–109	Dictionaries, Encyclopedias

notes are crucial for letting people know about strengths that cross over the boundaries of lines or are part of a line.

One of the 161 Music Conspectus lines is shown in table 3 as it would look online (available as a public file on RLIN, the Research Libraries Information Network), including information from all of the reporting institutions. Notice how the notes help you understand the characteristics of different collections, such as Berkeley's note linking the strengths of scores and sound recordings or Northwestern's note on a difference in collecting pre-20th-Century scores.

Even though LCC numbers are used to define the Music Conspectus, each Conspectus line represents the *subject* defined by the appropriate LCC class, and should not be strictly interpreted as only material that has actually been classified there. The Conspectus lines are linked to LCC classes as a matter of convenience and

Table 2: Codes Used In The Music Conspectus

0 = OUT OF SCOPE
   The library does not collect in this area.

1 = MINIMAL LEVEL
   A subject area in which few selections are made beyond very basic works.

2 = BASIC INFORMATION LEVEL
   A collection of up-to-date general materials that serve to introduce and
   define a subject and to indicate the varieties of information available
   elsewhere.

3 = INSTRUCTIONAL SUPPORT LEVEL
   A collection that is adequate to support undergraduate and most graduate
   instruction, or sustained independent study.

4 = RESEARCH LEVEL
   A collection that includes the major published source materials required
   for dissertations and independent research.

5 = COMPREHENSIVE LEVEL
   A collection in which a library endeavors, so far as is reasonably possible,
   to include all significant works of recorded knowledge.

For Books & Scores:
E = English language material predominates.
F = Selected foreign language material included.
W = Wide selection of material in all applicable languages.
Y = Material is primarily in one foreign language.

For Sound Recordings:
A = Major U.S. and European labels easily obtainable from American dealers.
B = Broad selection of North American labels and European direct imports.
C = Wide selection of commercial recordings issued throughout the world.

additional clarification of the subject or subjects encompassed there.
This means that libraries using other classification systems can
participate in the Conspectus by using equivalency charts or by
evaluating their holdings that have been assigned appropriate subject headings. Libraries that use the LCC system must likewise
treat the Conspectus lines as subject definitions, allowing for local
variants in using the scheme and for materials that might logically
fall in more than one place. For example, an institution with world-
class holdings in coconut shell scores classed as percussion might
reflect the presence of that collection in the Conspectus lines for

Table 3: Values In Music Conspectus Line 16
(Chamber Music, Scores)

(MUS16) MUSIC—INSTRUMENTAL MUSIC   PCR:None
Chamber Ensembles—Trios—Nonets and Larger Combinations
of Purely Chamber Music   M300–986

INSTITUTION	ECS/CCI	NOTES	
UC Santa Barbara	3/3	(3873)	Music Dept. Performance Library contains large # of chamber music parts.
Colorado State	2/2	(49)	
USC	3/3		
Stanford	3F/3F		
(2842)			
Yale	4/4F	(5609)	
UC Berkeley	4W/4W	(7440)	Strong collection of sound recordings.
UC Davis	3F/3F		ECS = 4F for string quartets; CIC = 4 for jazz transcriptions, 4W for post-1900 concert music.
UC Irvine	3/3	(2325)	
UCLA	4/4	(5162)	
UC Riverside	3/3	(1643)	
UC San Diego	3/3	(2669)	CCI = 4 for 20th century music.
UC Santa Cruz	3/3	(1482)	
LC	4/4W		
Miami	3/3W		Scores with more than 9 parts kept in Ensemble Library — not included in shelflist count.
Emory	1/1		
Iowa	3/3		
Northwestern	4/5	(5067)	Pre-20th century 3/3.
Notre Dame	4/4F	(604)	
Indiana	4W/4W		
Purdue	3F/3F		
Louisiana State	3/3		
Tulane	2/2F		
AAS	0/0		
Johns Hopkins	3/3	(2120)	Sound recordings 3/3.
Michigan State	3/3		Strong in woodwind quintets.

Table 3: *continued*

Michigan	3W/3W	(2545)	Includes rare book material.
Minnesota	3/3		
Dartmouth	2/3F	(1648)	
Princeton	3/3		
Rutgers	3F/3F	(841)	
SUNY Albany	2/2E		
SUNY Buffalo	4/4	(4242)	Includes duets (MUS11 and MUS15).
Columbia	3/3F	(2288)	
Cornell	3/3F	(3699)	
NYPL	4/4W		Black and American: 5W. Recordings: 5W.
NYU	2/3	(1206)	
Oklahoma	1/1F	(428)	
Penn State	3/3		
Temple	2/2	(868)	
Penn	3/3W		
Brown	2/4F		
British Library	4/4		
BYU	3F/3F	(309)	Music Department Performance Library.
Virginia	3F/3F		

both percussion music and national musics. In short, the Conspectus allows a subject specialist to sum up a wide variety of information about a collection in simple values in a chart.

HISTORY

The Music Conspectus was one of the earliest projects (and products) of the Research Libraries Group's Music Program Committee, which had its first official meeting in New Haven at the

Music Library Association's 50th anniversary meeting in 1981. RLG as a whole was in the process of creating portions of the Conspectus in many different subject areas at the time, and the Music Program Committee joined in. Like all the other subject areas then, the LCC was chosen as the basis for the Music Conspectus, although from the start the group believed that something different would be required for sound recordings. Paula Morgan of Princeton and Mike Keller (then at Cornell) worked on devising the breakdown of LCC classes into lines for the Conspectus, and in 1981 and 1982 a number of RLG institutions contributed values for the Music Conspectus.

These pioneers in assigning values to various parts of their collections were necessarily using their own subjective interpretations of what the definitions for levels 0 to 5 actually meant in terms of music collections. The directions for completing the Conspectus included suggestions for comparing holdings to standardized bibliographies and scanning the shelflist, but even then, in order to get the process started at all, people simply had to state their carefully considered opinions on the various strengths and weaknesses of their collections. As might have been expected (and as happened in other parts of the Conspectus as well) when the Music Conspectus values were submitted and compared, a great deal of discussion ensued. Much of the discussion centered on whether or not people's individual interpretations of the levels were comparable. That is, did one institution's "3" equal another institution's "3"? If two music librarians were both wavering between assigning a "2" or a "3", or a "3" vs. a "4" to a Conspectus line, did they make their final decisions based on the same elements? The numbers represented a continuum of possibilities, and placing those numbers into the continuum was a process that begged for cooperation and discussion if indeed there was to be any comparability from one institution's Conspectus values to another's.

Therefore, the Music Program Committee agreed to conduct a "verification study" to begin to verify that the values in the Conspectus were comparable. In other subjects, verification studies were taking the form of searching titles that appeared in standard bibliographies or searching periodicals indexed in a standard tool. These methods are very labor intensive and by necessity have been completed for only a very few Conspectus lines. Instead, the music verification study took the form of a shelflist measurement that could include every line in the entire Music Conspectus. It was conducted mostly in 1982, with the intent of studying ECS values. Since we had used LCC classes for the basis of the Music Conspectus, anyone with a shelflist in LCC could easily measure and count to get an estimate of the number of titles that had been classified in the LCC numbers assigned to each line of the Conspectus.

A purely quantitative study obviously could not take into account all of the information that resulted in the assignment of ECS levels.[6] Nevertheless, the verification study could suggest areas in which the values looked unusual and might benefit from reexamination or, even better, explanation in a note. The result did not mandate certain quantitative levels that would override the expert's opinion, although suggestions of appropriate quantities were first distributed in 1983 and later revised in 1987 by the Music Program Committee.

It took a great deal of courage for the Music Program Committee to conduct this shelflist count—to expose our raw numbers to each other and risk having our faculty find out that we had 200 fewer piano scores than a similar institution down the road or across town. On the other hand, putting those shelflist counts into the body of the Conspectus (they are the numbers in parentheses at the beginning of the notes fields) substantially helped a lot of people who participated in the Conspectus later to make informed decisions about what levels they would assign. I just hope they didn't limit the levels they assigned to an interpretation of those counts.

Music remains the only part of the Conspectus that has a shelflist count associated with it.

After most of the Music Program Committee had completed the shelflist counts, attention turned to attempting to describe our sound recordings collections in the Conspectus. It seemed like a good idea to describe the strengths of the individual sound recordings collections within the consortium, but finding a way to represent those strengths was difficult. Whatever your complaints about the limitations of the LCC classification system for describing strengths in books and scores, it cannot be denied that it was easy to go to the shelflist (in those pre-online catalog days when we had accurate shelflists!) and look over the cards in each classification. You might find a new pattern of holdings you hadn't been aware of, or confirm a previously held notion that a lot in "X" field had been purchased over the last few years, but it was possible to scan and evaluate the holdings in a convenient manner. Where were the parallels for sound recording collections that were rarely classified in any way?

After much discussion among the Music Program Committee it was finally agreed that because of the make-up of participating institutions in that group, we could *assume* we all had core collections of Western art music, and what we really wanted to know about each other was what we had *besides* that. Thus, a simple recordings Conspectus was devised that lumped standard classical music repertoire into just one line, then added 21 more lines on various styles of music, ranging from jazz to the music of Southeast Asia. One line from the recordings portion of the Conspectus is depicted in table 4 as it would appear online. Again, see how helpful the notes are in giving a sense of what's important, unusual, or somehow notable about a collection. SUNY Buffalo's indication of a different level of collecting for a particular segment (in this case "rock music") seems very helpful, as does Brigham Young's note concerning the KEYY archive.

Table 4: Values In Music Conspectus Line 145
(Popular Music, Sound Recordings)

(MUS145) MUSIC—SOUND RECORDINGS   PCR:None
(Western, commercial music)   Popular Music

INSTITUTION	ECS/CCI	NOTES
UC Santa Barbara	2/2	
Colorado State	0/0	
USC	2/2	In College Library.
Stanford	0/0	
Yale	1A/0	
UC Berkeley	0/2A	
UC Irvine	0/0	
UCLA	3/3	(15,000) Includes 8,000 LPs, 5,000 78s, 200 cylinders, 1800 other in APAM.
UC Riverside	1/1	
UC San Diego	3/2	
UC Santa Cruz	1/1	
LC	4/5C	Armed Forces Radio and Television Service Collection and NBC Radio Collection strong in post-1930 pop.
Miami	1/1A	
Emory	1/1	
Iowa	1/1	
Northwestern	4B/4B	
Notre Dame	2/1A	
Indiana	0/1A	
Purdue	0/0	
Louisiana State	2B/2	
AAS	0/0	
Johns Hopkins	0/0	
Michigan	1A/1A	
Minnesota	1/1	
Dartmouth	2A/3A	
Princeton	0/0	
Rutgers	0/0	
SUNY Buffalo	2A/2A	4B for history of rock music. Most others are gifts or cut-outs.
Cornell	2/2A	Only U.S. labels.

Table 4: *Continued*

NYPL	4A/4B	Good collection of popular music from 1930's-1950's in Schomburg: CCI = 5B
NYU	0/0	
Penn State	1A/1A	
Temple	2A/0	
Penn	0/0	
British Library	0/0	
BYU	4B/3B	The KEYY library contains a nearly complete set of Capitol Records releases and many popular artists of the 50's and 60's.
Virginia	1/1	

There have been many complaints about the sound recordings Conspectus, both inside and outside RLG. It is true that it does not give the same level of detail about a library's overall recordings collection as the rest of the Conspectus does for other materials. It must be remembered that it was designed as a compromise to be used by a small group of libraries with relatively similar collections.

In the mid-1980's there came a diminution in Conspectus activity within RLG's Music Program Committee. People had grown tired of discussing it at every meeting, the dollar was strong, economic times were better, and the prospect of being forced to do serious cooperative projects in collection development had faded. There were several attempts in the latter 1980's to undertake more narrow verification projects involving searching bibliographies (including one on chamber music headed by Kären Nagy for which the searching was actually completed), but none has yet been reflected in the Conspectus itself. Up until this point, the Music Conspectus had been considered a work-in-progress, with a group actively suggesting ways in which it could be improved. With the dissolution of RLG's Music Program Committee in spring 1989, the most direct forum for additional work on the Music Conspectus disappeared.

APPLICATIONS AND USE

In order to find out other people's appraisals of the Music Conspectus and what it has meant at the institutional level, in December 1990-January 1991 I conducted a survey of people who had contributed values to the Music Conspectus online. There were usable responses from twenty-five people (mainly music librarians).[7]

The responses indicated that music librarians were generally responsible for filling out the Conspectus values for their collections and have used their personal knowledge of the collections to accomplish this. Although seventeen respondents thought that the Conspectus values accurately represented their collections, it is clear that the Conspectus does not play an important role in music selectors' daily activities. In the first place, the Conspectus is consulted infrequently: many more people stated they consult the Conspectus "yearly" or "never" than any other response. Furthermore, only two people thought the Music Conspectus was "extremely useful," while four called it "somewhat useful;" eleven said it was "not very useful."

Nonetheless, there were people who found uses for Conspectus information for particular projects. Six people said they had been able to identify areas of their collections that were weak through the Conspectus. Four people pointed out the usefulness of citing peer institutions' values (particularly shelflist counts) to bolster arguments for increased funding of the music budget or specific parts of it. And three reported that they had used the Conspectus as a foundation to build on in writing collection development policy statements.

In my own experience, the shelflist count and discussions on the results of it took place shortly after I arrived at the University of Michigan. Although I hadn't assigned the original Conspectus values, the shelflist measurement project and subsequent follow-ups were an excellent introduction to my new collection. My experience verified the statement, "The skills of the librarians who participate in the conspectus process are upgraded."[8] One of the respondents to my survey similarly stated, "the greatest usefulness [of the conspectus] was the process of completing it." Moreover, I was also one of the people who discovered weaknesses in my collection through the shelflist measurement project. I'm sure I would have eventually become aware of those weaknesses myself in the normal course of my work without the benefit of the Conspectus or the verification project, but the information in the shelflist count in particular was concrete and specific. There were areas I could point to and say "we're supporting our programs as well as our peers are doing here," but there were others in which I could point to Conspectus lines and say "we have DMA programs in these areas but we don't have as many scores to support them as do other institutions who have no degree programs in the area." That was a successful argument and I, like others, got funds to build those areas up.

Whatever use or disuse the Conspectus found among music librarians, it must be recognized that the Conspectus framework became the *lingua franca* of general collection development in the 1980's. Outside of RLG, the Conspectus spread rapidly. In the early to mid-1980's it was adopted as the vehicle for the Association of Research Libraries' (ARL) North American Collections Inventory Project (NCIP) and suddenly large libraries all over the country were looking intensely at this tool. Several ARL libraries in the state of Indiana completed a pilot project and deemed the Conspectus usable.[9] Colorado and Alaska had statewide Conspectus projects, the seven University of California campuses and several Illinois institutions completed the Conspectus, a consortium of libraries in the Northwest used it, and the New York state and METRO projects are using it, as is the National Library of Canada. Conspectus studies are also underway or being considered in England, Scotland, Australia, and Sweden.

Yet, despite all the accolades the Conspectus has received, the music librarians I surveyed and talked to generally don't like it and haven't found it very useful. The most frequently cited complaint is that the subject lines based on LCC classes do not represent useful categories that would be used in collection evaluation and development. The LCC classes and shelflist measurement clearly are means to a quick overview of music collections, but that does not give information that is parallel to the way in which we normally build our collections or might otherwise identify strong and weak points in the collection. I'll leave it to Lenore Coral to go further into these questions, but will summarize my evaluation of the Music Conspectus as a tool:

I believe the Conspectus as it currently stands is a framework that can provide a beginning point for us successfully to evaluate our collections. The simplicity and convenience of being able to measure a shelflist is one of the cheapest ways of achieving this. It is quick and dirty, and its results have to be seen as such. They are a very preliminary product. The nature of what we buy and why we buy it for one particular collection is not always easy to analyze; it is even harder to compare what we buy and why to what is done in other collections. That is why some quantifiable aspects of the collections are welcome. Other quantifiable projects are possible, of course, and some of them are getting more likely every day. The computer-aided means of comparing and evaluating collections will surely become the norm when our collections are fully converted to machine-readable cataloging.

The Conspectus is the common language of collection evaluation at this time. This doesn't mean that the Music Conspectus has to stay the way it is if we can find a better way of doing it. For instance, the Conspectus is not mandated to be linked to LCC classes, and different definitions of Conspectus lines might improve it. The model itself could accommodate changes that would make it more appealing to music librarians. The difficulty is that with the

RLG Music Program Committee dissolved and use of the conspectus spreading, it is now unclear who has the responsibility or the power to change it.

I leave this challenge with the Music Library Association: it is up to music librarians to make the Music Conspectus a tool that works for us. If there are to be improvements to the Music Conspectus, it is up to us to suggest them and work to have them adopted.

References and Notes

1. Nancy E. Gwinn and Paul H. Mosher, "Coordinating Collection Development: The RLG Conspectus," *College and Research Libraries* 44 (1983):128.

2. Anthony W. Ferguson, Joan Grant, and Joel S. Rutstein, "The RLG Conspectus: Its Uses and Benefits," *College and Research Libraries* 49 (1988):198.

3. Richard M. Dougherty, "A Conceptual Framework for Organizing Resource Sharing and Shared Collection Development Programs," *Journal of Academic Librarianship* 14 (1988):290.

4. Conversation with L. Yvonne Wulff, Assistant Director for Collection Development, University of Michigan, February 1991.

5. Collection Management and Development Committee, Research Libraries Group, Minutes of meeting, Nov. 7–8, 1985. "I. Using Overlap Data," p. 3.

6. For example, one institution holding 500 scores of a specialized nature, such as mandolin solos, might have given an ECS of 4 to the appropriate Conspectus line because for mandolin solos they had a collection strong enough to support research. Another library might hold 1,000 scores more evenly distributed across the classes of the same Conspectus line and assign a level 3 because their collection would not support in-depth research in those fields.

7. See the Appendix for a summary of selected questions and responses.

8. Larry R. Oberg, "Evaluating the Conspectus Approach for Smaller Library Collections," *College and Research Libraries* 49 (1988):195.

9. In that project Indiana University independently modified the Music Conspectus by breaking down the lines into smaller pieces.

APPENDIX

SAMPLE OF RESULTS FROM QUESTIONNAIRE
ON THE RLG MUSIC CONSPECTUS

NOTE: This questionnaire was distributed in December 1990–
January 1991 to people whose institutions had contributed values
to the Music Conspectus. Twenty-five usable responses were received. The author wishes to thank those who participated.

1. Who filled in the values for the Music Conspectus in your institution?

    music librarian   23
    CD officer   2*
    other   2*

    *Each including 1 in collaboration with a music librarian.

2. How were values for the Music Conspectus lines determined for
your institution?

    personal knowledge of the collection   19
    examination of the shelflist   12
    examination of subject headings   0
    all of the above   2
    don't know   2
    other   2

3. Did you change any values in the Conspectus for your music collection as a result of the shelflist count?

    Yes   11
    No   4

4. Do you feel the present values for music in the Conspectus are
an accurate representation of your collection?

    Yes   17
    No   4
    Don't know   2
    Not sure   1

5a. How often do you consult the Conspectus?

>Weekly   0
>
>Monthly   1
>
>Few times a year   7
>
>Yearly   10
>
>Never   5

5b. Do you most often consult it in paper or online?

>Paper   16
>
>Online   1

5c. Have you ever consulted it online?

>Yes   6
>
>No   15

6. Overall, how would you rank the usefulness of the Music Conspectus?

>Extremely useful   2
>
>Moderately useful   4
>
>Somewhat useful   5
>
>Not very useful   11
>
>Useless   1

Guidelines for Evaluating Music Collections as Part of a Regional Assessment Plan

Elizabeth Davis

ABSTRACT: METRO (New York Metropolitan Reference and Research Organization) is involved in an ongoing Collection Inventory Project. Modeled on a similar regional project in the Pacific Northwest, the METRO plan uses Conspectus worksheets to record information from libraries in the region. The METRO Music Task Force was formed to develop a verification document, or "Supplemental Guidelines" for evaluating music collections in the region. The guidelines divide the field of music by format, and recommend published bibliographies (or "benchmarks") that can be used to check holdings of books, periodicals, scores, and sound recordings.

METRO (New York Metropolitan Reference and Research Organization) is the name given to a consortium of libraries formed to share resources, staff, expertise, and institutional experience for the mutual benefit of its members. It provides a forum for all types of libraries—academic, school, public, and special—to engage in common activities. In addition, it has created formal resource sharing networks through which individual users from one library can have access to other members' libraries.

METRO invites representatives of member libraries to work on its various committees. One of these committees, its Resources Development Committee, is engaged in an ongoing "Collections Inventory

Elizabeth Davis is Music Librarian at Columbia University. She is responsible for collection development and evaluation of music materials at Columbia, and was a member of METRO's Music Task Force on Supplemental Guidelines for evaluating music collections. She is presently Chair of MLA's Resource Sharing and Collection Development Committee.

Project."[1] This project, which had its formal beginnings in 1987, is designed to meet two goals. The first is to improve the management of collection-building by supporting a regional assessment of member collections by subject, and recording the results of that assessment in a database. The second is to use the database to assist with cooperative collection development and sharing agreements that would selectively coordinate collection growth and strengthen the combined subject resources in the region.

The method of recording the assessment data follows the traditional Conspectus format. Although the Conspectus tool was initially developed by the Research Libraries Group for its members, other groups with different focuses have adopted this approach. When designing its program, METRO adopted, with some major adaptations, the work of another regional model, that of the Library Resources for the Northwest (LIRN). Like METRO, this group serves as an umbrella organization for all types of libraries in a single geographical region. From LIRN's program, METRO was able to incorporate the worksheets, training materials, and manual for its own use.

In conjunction with Conspectus assignments, METRO members are introduced to a number of assessment verification techniques. These include list-checking against an authoritative list of publications, commonly referred to as "Supplemental Guidelines." (Other techniques include shelf scanning, shelflist measurement, citation analysis, and evaluation by an outside expert.) Where possible, the RLG Supplemental Guidelines for particular subject areas were adapted. For subjects where no guidelines are provided by RLG, notably Music and History, METRO organized local committees to develop them. It was for this purpose that the METRO Music Task Force was formed in July 1989.[2] The group provided a good representation of the member libraries who would be participating in the program. The charge of the Music Task Force was to design supplemental guidelines in music for use with the METRO

Collection Inventory Project. These guidelines were to consist of assessment tools or "benchmarks" to be used as a means of verifying our individual Conspectus assignments and to help bibliographers in setting the levels of their collections.

In order to survey the music terrain, the group divided the field by format into sound recordings, scores, periodicals, and books. The inclusion of nonprint materials in our collections on a fundamental level provided one impetus for this decision. In their role as primary sound documentation for both the western and non-western musical traditions, recordings are critically important. In addition, they serve an important pedagogical purpose, enabling performers to study a wide range of techniques and interpretation for all kinds of music. Pragmatically, many of the music collections of the METRO libraries might contain only recordings for study and recreational listening.

In covering print materials, it seemed logical to examine scores as a separate subset. Like recordings, these serve as primary documents for the transmission of notated music. Their specific notational language further reinforces their separateness, causing them in many cases to be housed apart from central collections. Additionally, in many collections, scores are classified according to specific music classification schemes. At the five institutions represented on the Task Force, three different systems are used to assign call numbers to scores (Juilliard and Columbia use versions of the Dickinson classification scheme; NYPL uses an in-house location class-mark; NYU and Brooklyn College use the Library of Congress *Classification*). Also, factors affecting patron use and preservation treatment of scores are specific to the format of the material.

With the remaining print materials, we felt that a further breakdown between periodicals and books was justified. Periodicals are, of course, important sources for current information. Generally, new subjects are introduced into the field through the periodical literature. Periodicals serve a wide variety of users, including the enthusiast, the generalist, and the specialist. In addition, the recent pricing schemes (or scams) for periodicals in general are forcing many libraries to treat them separately from the rest of the collection for budgetary reasons. Because of these considerations, periodicals constitute a primary category of material for resource sharing (i.e., sharing subscriptions among consortia members) as well as interlibrary loan activity (the shorter lengths of articles makes them more suitable for photocopying than monographs). Both of these activities would be very useful by-products of the assessment process.

Books require a separate focus. They form the core of our collections and continue to be the primary means of transmission of knowledge for humanistic subjects. In format, they match the materials for other subjects in our collections. We all know from experience that our administrators are more comfortable when we can move to discussions of books, after dealing with scores and recordings.

Each task force member chose a format, studied the potentially available tools, and presented recommendations. Eventually we settled on a core list of "benchmarks" and for each benchmark, a sampling method. We all searched each of the tools against our collections. In some cases, we searched the entire work; in others we took a random sampling.

These benchmarks represent the bibliographies and discographies that, at this stage, best match the purpose and structure of the METRO Conspectus. The list of benchmark sources (with their full bibliographic citations) chosen for this project, along with indications of the Conspectus levels they can be used to assess, are given in the appendix to this paper. (These sources will be referred to by their short titles throughout the rest of this paper.)

In many ways, books proved to be the most problematic area to describe. Since western art music is based on European antecedents, much of the literature concerns those antecedents. Not only the primary literature, but a large amount of the secondary literature in the field, is published in languages other than English. This is less problematic in the lower levels where there is primary reliance on English-language holdings. Adequate representation is likely to be found in the general literature, including *Books for College Libraries*, *The Reader's Adviser*, and the *Guide to Reference Books*.

Difficulties lie in testing for foreign-language coverage that becomes crucial at mid-level collecting. To provide this coverage, the bibliographies in *The New Grove* were examined. Because of the overlap of titles across articles, however, it was difficult to identify a satisfactory sampling strategy. The article on "Schubert" was chosen, and every title in the bibliography was searched.

However, further limitations were encountered. Some were simply annoying—the bibliographies are printed in small type and difficult to read—but others were conceptually self-limiting. Book and periodical article citations are listed in one sequence, so one must first edit the list to make it useful. The chronological arrangement, which may work well enough in the shorter bibliographies, can cause problems in the longer listings, where there may be further sub-arrangements. Such an arrangement can hinder searching in an alphabetically-arranged card catalog. Despite these practical difficulties, it seems likely that these lists have the potential to be the most useful for assessing book titles in collections at level 3 and above. For additional foreign-language coverage, a useful, but now outdated list is the *International Basic List*; for currency, the *Notes* "Books Recently Published" column provides essential coverage.

For periodicals, the lists in *Magazines for Libraries* and "Current Periodicals" chapter in *Music: A Guide to the Reference Literature* provide effective coverage for assessing levels 1–3. *Music Index*, which covers the principal areas of music, can be used for mid- and upper-levels. Not included in the supplemental guidelines are the many specialized indexes, for example, *Music Psychology Index*, *Jazz Index*,[3] or other retrospective indexes, which would be relevant for research and comprehensive collections. The "Periodicals" list in *The New Grove* is a formidable one, describing a significant portion of the universe of music periodicals, and is a required tool for more intensive collecting levels. As with the other formats, keeping current through the periodical literature itself is essential.

The primary assessment tool for scores is *Basic Music Library*, published under the auspices of the Music Library Association. It is designed for the building of basic collections and focuses on the standard repertory. Its principal drawback is its publication date. A revision, which will include scores and recordings, is currently in progress under the auspices of the Music Library Association's Resource Sharing and Collection Development Committee. Also, it was decided in using this work, that we not limit ourselves to the edition specified, even though that edition was thought to be the best one available at the time the book was published. We do, however, believe that specifying edition is particularly important for performance considerations.

We cover the increasingly-important area of score facsimiles with "A Checklist of Music Manuscripts" (Abravanel, updated by Coover). For historical sets, we looked to use two sources: *Historical Sets, Collected Editions* and the "Editions, historical" article (from *The New Grove*). This latter bibliography has good coverage of score anthologies. However, we were taken aback (and our schedule slowed) when we found the collected historical editions listed alphabetically by first word of the title, including indefinite article.

In sampling *Historical Sets, Collected Editions*, we all checked every fourth series title, agreeing that if a single title from the series was in the collection, the series was considered to be in the collection. One of us checked every title, in addition, and the difference in percentages was notable—roughly 30% for sampling vs. 4% for complete checking. This discrepancy cast some doubt on our reliance on the sampling methodology. And, finally, the *Notes* "Music Received" column is required for comprehensive, up-to-date coverage.

Identifying appropriate assessment tools for sound recordings presents a significant challenge. If a score collection is present, it is likely that a library will want to see a close and complementary relationship between its scores and sound recordings. An exact match will be difficult to achieve, as most libraries do not have sound archives that might contain recordings that were never released commercially. For repertory not represented by scores, such correlation is, of course, not possible.

The tools used for scores can also be used for assessing recordings, with some caveats. Particular performances, analogous to specific score editions, would not be specified. Non-notated musics would not be covered.

In using the discographical literature, we found the discographies to be numerous and to vary widely in scope and format. They tend to be organized on one or more criteria, e.g., composer, performing artist, medium, or nationality, and the entries are then treated selectively or exhaustively according to that criteria. We could not identify a satisfactory comprehensive listing comparable to the score listings in *Basic Music Library*.

In order to focus the assessments using the discographical literature, we divide sound recordings by repertory into three different areas: western classical, jazz/popular, and world music.

For western classical music, the distinction between composition and performance may be important. For while we might all agree that recordings of the Beethoven symphonies are essential, the choice of performers is apt to be based on the individual discography compiler's preference, rather than on a broad or scholarly consensus.

This individual approach to compilation is evident in examining the discographies listed. "A Basic Stock List" divides a core list of 400 compositions into primary and secondary tiers, but makes no recommendations as to specific recordings. *A Basic Classical and Operatic Recordings Collection* ranks pieces into three Conspectus-like tiers. Halsey's approach in his *Classical Music*

Recordings is interesting for its division of works into 11 categories, but we did not find his eccentric 5-point rating system useful for our purposes.

The selective discographies chosen for both world music and the jazz/popular categories might best be viewed as general guides to artists, styles, and historical developments rather than as canonical tabulations of specific recordings. In world music, *Musics of the World* carries the cachet of being assembled by UCLA music faculty and graduate students with the appropriate expertise. The discographies published annually in the journal *Ethnomusicology* provide worldwide coverage and are broadly inclusive of ethnic classical, traditional, folk, and popular musics. The tools selected for the jazz-/popular areas cover a wide variety of musics, including jazz, rock, musicals, country/western, and new age in the formats likely to be found in most libraries, namely, albums, singles, and LPs. Although we have identified benchmarks for sound recordings for this particular project, it appears to us that the larger question of assessing recorded sound collections should be revisited on a larger, and perhaps, national, scale.

Having outlined the assessment tools, let me now give two examples of how we expect them to correlate to collection levels. The standard six collecting levels currently defined by ALA are: out of scope, minimal, basic information, instructional support, research, and comprehensive.

Excluding out of scope, or zero, the levels at either end, 1 and 5, minimal and comprehensive, are self-explanatory; they define collections with almost nothing to collections with almost everything. The instructional level, at level 3, serves as the middlepoint of reference. Some tools, for example, *Basic Music Library* are specifically designed to describe a level-3, or instructional-level collection.

Let us focus on the two levels that tend to be somewhat fluid and more difficult to identify: levels 2 and 4, the first a basic information collection and level 4, a research collection.

A basic information level collection serves to introduce and define the subject and to indicate the varieties of information available elsewhere. Such a collection is not expected to support sustained independent study; nor does it imply a strong reference collection. What one is likely to find at this level is a visible presence of music materials in the collection.

For books, the collection contains substantial holdings from *The Humanities*, as well as *The Reader's Adviser*. For bibliographers wishing to enhance their basic level collections by providing information on a wider range of topics and with more depth, but without striving to level 3, a significant number of titles from *Books for College Libraries* and *Music: A Guide to the Reference Literature*'s listing of reference books should be present. For periodicals, most titles listed in *Magazines for Libraries* and some additional representation from *Music: A Guide to the Reference Literature* are included.

For scores, a good representation of titles from *Basic Music Library*, including score anthologies covering all historical periods are found.

For recordings in the western classical tradition, the level-2 collection contains a substantial majority of core repertory. It contains a representative, though necessarily selective view of significant styles and genres, with a minimal inclusion of secondary figures and multiple performances. Where applicable, a correlation to scores is assumed. It would include up to approximately half of the entries in "A Basic stock list" and *Basic Classical and Operatic Recordings Collection*.

For world music, the collection would include a representative, but selective overview of major regions and ethnic groups of the world, with up to half the titles in *Musics of the World*. Reliance on commercial U.S. or western European issues is assumed. For jazz/popular, a balanced coverage of the major genres is assumed. One would find only the most important artists, and few of them would be represented by more than one recording. Up to approximately half of the titles in *Essential Jazz Records, The Development of Library Collections of Sound Recordings*, or *The Popular Music Handbook* may be found.

Within the METRO consortia, we might expect to find a basic level collection at a four-year college with survey courses and courses in music appreciation, or in a small public library.

Moving to research level 4, we would expect to find collections that move beyond mere support to those utilized for sustained independent study. Their resources would contain the major published source materials required for dissertations and independent research, but without the archival or special collections characteristic of comprehensive collections. Works in many specialized areas, monographic series, broad foreign language holdings, and imprints from all major world regions, particularly Europe, are assumed, as is a notably strong reference collection.

For reference literature, a high proportion of monograph titles in *Music Reference and Research Materials* and *Information on Music* should be included. The general monographic literature would cover a majority of the titles (in all languages) cited in the bibliographies in *The New Grove*. For periodicals, most titles listed in *Music Index*, relevant to those areas of concern to or taught in the parent institution should be found. Significant numbers of titles listed in the "Periodicals" article (from *The New Grove*) should also be found. Also represented are titles from both the retrospective and subject bibliographies, as well as specialized indexes, depending upon the institution's mission.

For scores, all titles in *Basic Music Library* are assumed. Coverage of titles in *Historical Sets, Collected Editions* is thorough, and the collection would include the national monumental sets and facsimile series. A strong representation of anthologies listed in "Editions, historical" (from *The New Grove*) is also found.

Recordings are represented by deep, systematic coverage in the three areas. Classical repertory would include composers and styles throughout music history, and performers throughout the era of sound recordings, with additional emphasis on selected areas that are of special interest to the institution, as defined by specialized discographies. Almost all titles in *Recorded Classical Music* would be found.

For jazz/popular, one would find major, secondary, and minor figures, schools, and genres. All titles in *The History of Rock and Roll* and *Jazz on Record*, as well as a significant number from *60 Years of Recorded Jazz* would appear. For world music, coverage of the world's regions and groups in particular areas of concentration would be represented with strong holdings from the ongoing *Ethnomusicology* bibliographies. Some non-commercial, pre-LP and 45 rpm recordings will be included, as well as field recordings in the areas of concentration.

Within the METRO consortium, level-4 ratings will be found in the university libraries and major conservatories.

There are some limitations and drawbacks to the guidelines we have proposed. They strongly emphasize western art music. The state of librarianship and bibliography for music outside of this tradition makes it difficult to identify or provide the necessary general prescriptive guidelines for its assessment. The guidelines, by definition, are static. Evaluation must be based on the best available bibliographies.

The emerging technologies are not addressed. Nowhere in the guidelines does one find tools to access holdings of machine-readable files, videos, or hypermedia products. We do expect to capture a library's holdings in these areas through a query on the Conspectus form, but only for informational purposes. It is too soon to assess the impact that the products based on these technologies will have on our collections and our users. It is METRO policy to rely only on published bibliographies for assessment projects. We did not include publishers' or dealers' lists, even though some of them reflect thorough and scholarly work. For example, monthly listings of scores provided by vendors such as Harrassowitz, as well as the informative catalogs of published facsimiles provided by Old Manuscripts and Incunabula, Inc. are important and useful products.

For libraries engaged in the process, the time needed for sampling is significant. Manual checking is required, much of it through catalogs in card format. Checking every score title in *Basic Music Library* took one bibliographer approximately 50 hours. If help is provided by non-musically trained personnel, results in scores and recordings checking may be difficult to trust.

However, the rewards are significant. As a bibliographer engaged in the process, one gets a much better knowledge of one's collections and is, thus, in a better position to serve users effectively. A bibliographer will also have a stronger basis in building and sharing knowledge with colleagues, as well as with administrators. For our specific needs, the METRO Collections Inventory Project will have a stronger database on which to build its activities.

Notes and References

1. This project is described in the *METRO Collection Inventory Project Manual*, prepared by METRO's Resources Development Committee, Collection Assessment Task Force (New York: METRO, 1991). The manual is available from the New York Metropolitan Reference and Research Library Agency, 57 East 11th Street, New York, NY 10003. Telephone: (212) 228-2320; FAX: (212) 228-2598.

2. Its members were: Jane Gottlieb, Head Librarian, The Juilliard School; Kent Underwood, Reference Librarian for Music, New York University; Honora Raphael, Music Librarian, Brooklyn College; and, Elizabeth Davis, Music Librarian, Columbia Univer-

sity. Robert Kenselaar of the New York Public Library chaired the group.

3. *Music Psychology Index.* [Denton, Texas]: Institute for Therapeutics Research, v. 2– ; 1978– . *Jazz Index.* [Frankfurt am Main]: N. Ruecker], Jahrg. 1–7, 1977–87.

APPENDIX: Bibliographic Tools Used in the Supplemental Guidelines for Music

BOOKS

Association of College & Research Libraries, comp., *Books for College Libraries: A Core Collection of 50,000 Titles.* 3d ed. Chicago: American Library Assn., 1988. 5 vols.

The music section (vol. 1, pp. 159–210) presents a classified list of 1,129 music books, virtually all in English, plus 23 score anthologies.

Level 1–4

Blazek, Ron and Elizabeth Aversa, T*he Humanities: A Selective Guide to Information Sources.* 3rd ed. Littleton, CO: Libraries Unlimited, 1988.

Music section (Chapter 10, pp. 178–218) cites 138 titles, almost all English-language, mainly reference works, but also including general histories of music.

Level 1–3

Brockman, William S., *Music: A Guide to the Reference Literature.* Littleton, CO: Libraries Unlimited, 1987.

Occupies a middle ground between *Books for College Libraries* and Duckles. Parts 1–5 describe a core reference collection of 559 titles.

Level 2–4

Charles, Sydney Robinson, *A Handbook of Music and Music Literature in Sets and Series.* New York: Free Press, 1972.

Section C (pp. 326–405) covers 82 monographs and facsimile series from Europe and the U.S., with full title-by-title listing.

Dated, but still valuable as a checklist.

Level 3–4

Duckles, Vincent H. and Michael A. Keller, *Music Reference and Research Materials: An Annotated Bibliography*. 4th ed. New York: Schirmer Books, 1988.

Though somewhat hobbled by haphazard editing, the 4th edition of this classic work provides an indispensable inventory of 3,212 reference works.

Level 3–4

Marco, Guy A., *Information on Music: A Handbook of Reference Sources in European Languages*. Littleton, CO: Libraries Unlimited, 1975–1984. 3 vols.

Designed to complement the 3rd ed. of Duckles (1974). Vol. I ("Basic and Universal Sources") lists 503 works. Vols. II–III ("The Americas" and "Europe") contain more than 3,000 citations; the vast majority are published monographs, but some articles and unpublished materials are also included.

Level 3–4

Music Library Association, comp., *Basic Music Library: Essential Scores and Books*. 2nd ed. Chicago: American Library Assn., 1983.

Designed primarily for music selection in general libraries. Books section lists 499 titles.

Level 1–3

Music Library Association, *Notes: the Quarterly Journal of the Music Library Association*. Canton, MA: Music Library Association, 1943-

Quarterly "Books Recently Published" columns list new monographs. In-depth coverage though limited largely to western languages and imprints and with less than comprehensive coverage of European books. Vol. 45 (1988–89) lists 1,017 titles (555 English, plus 462 non-English); Vol. 46 (1989–90) lists 945 titles (531 English, plus 414 non-English).

Level 1–4

Public Libraries Commission, International Association of Music Libraries, ed. *International Basic List of Literature on Music.* Den Haag: Nederlands Bibliotheek en Lectuur Centrum, 1975.
Lists about 500 titles, not limited to reference books, with an international, multilingual perspective.
Level 2–3

The Reader's Adviser: A Layman's Guide to Literature. 13th ed. New York: Bowker, 1988. 5 vols.
The music section, contributed by Michael Keller (vol. 3, pp. 484–518) provides an up-to-date and well-rounded list of some 400 titles, all in English.
Level 1–3

Sadie, Stanley, ed., *The New Grove Dictionary of Music and Musicians.* London: Macmillan, 1980. 20 vols.
The standard English-language encyclopedic music reference source.
Level 3–4

Sheehy, Eugene, ed., *Guide to Reference Books.* 10th ed. Chicago: American Library Assn., 1986.
Reference works only. The music section (pp. 599–627) with 353 citations, is wide-ranging yet superbly selective so as to provide a useful measure even at the research level, while an introductory paragraph (p. 599) addresses the minimal needs of small general libraries.
Level 1–4

Winesanker, Michael, *A List of Books on Music.* Reston, VA: National Association of Schools of Music, 1977.
A project of the National Association of Schools of Music in consultation with the Music Library Association, and designed expressly as a core collection for music schools. Lists 157 reference works and 1,140 other books on music.
Level 2–4

PERIODICALS

Brockman, William S., *Music: A Guide to the Reference Literature.*
(For complete citation, see Books section)
"Current periodicals" section (pp. 161–85) includes 110 American and European journals. Though numerically similar to *Magazines for Libraries* (see below), Brockman's selection is oriented more towards the music specialist.
Level 2–3

Fellinger, Imogen, "Periodicals," in Stanley S. Sadie, ed. *The New Grove Dictionary.* (For complete citation, see Books section).
Vol. 14, pp. 407–535.
Comprehensive listing of over 6,000 periodicals, both current and historical, geographically arranged. Includes alphabetical index.
Level 4

Fidler, Linda and Richard S. James, *International Music Journals.*
Westport, CT: Greenwood, 1990.
Covers 81 periodicals, dating from 1798–1983, selected for their importance to music research.
Level 3–4

Katz, William A., *Magazines for Libraries.* 6th ed. New York: Bowker, 1989.
"Music Periodicals" (pp. 799–814) includes 96 English-language titles in three categories: general, popular, reviews and listings (i.e., of sound recordings). With a rich selection of non-specialist periodicals, this is a good source for the general collection.
Level 1–3

Music Index. Warren, MI: Harmonie Park Press, 1949- .
As of 1990, includes over 375 current periodicals. International in scope. New journals listed separately at their first appearance in the index.
Level 2–4

Music Library Association, comp. *Basic Music Library.*
    Lists 61 periodicals, divided into three collecting levels.
    Level 1–3

Music Library Association, *Notes.* (For complete citation, see Books
    section)
    "New Periodicals" column includes report on new journals.
    Level 1–4

Pruett, James W. and Thomas B. Slavens, *Research Guide to Musi-
    cology.* Chicago: American Library Assn., 1985.
    "Annotated listing of selected music periodicals" (pp. 141–46)
    covers 16 academic journals.
    Level 3

Robinson, Doris S., *Music and Dance Periodicals: An International
    Directory and Guidebook.* Voorheesville, NY: Peri, 1989.
    The most extensive single listing of currently published music
    periodicals worldwide; excluding those that pertain specifically to
    dance, there are more than 1,700 titles.
    Level 4

Winesanker, Michael, *A List of Books on Music.* (For complete cita-
    tion, see Books section)
    Appendix offers select list of 51 periodicals, specifically chosen
    for their appropriateness to music-school libraries.
    Level 2–3

SCORES

Abravanel, Claude, "A Checklist of Music Manuscripts in Facsimile
    Edition" *Notes* 34 (1978), pp. 557–70, Supplement by James
    Coover, *Notes* 37 (1981), pp. 533–56.

Together, these cover 456 facsimile editions. "Although the compilation . . . is not exhausive, it is representative of the facsimiles that have appeared since the middle of the nineteenth century." Supplemented since 1981 by "Music Received" columns in *Notes* (see below).
Level 3–4

Association of College & Research Libraries, comp., *Books for College Libraries.*
Includes small selection of music anthologies (23 titles), appropriate to general collections.
Level 1–2

Charles, Syndey Robinson, "Editions, historical," in *The New Grove*, v. 5, pp. 848–69.
A selection of 937 titles, including 282 single-composer collected editions, 180 other collected editions (e.g., monuments, etc.), 20 collected editions of theoretical works, and 455 miscellaneous anthologies.
Level 3–4

Heyer, Anna Harriet, *Historical Sets, Collected Editions, and Monuments of Music.* 3rd ed. Chicago: American Library Assn., 1980. 2 vols.
Covers about 1,300 series, broadly inclusive of composers' collected works, historical and monumental sets, and performing series.
Level 3–4

Music Library Association, comp., *Basic Music Library.*
Designed as a tool for building basic music collections in general libraries, it includes 1,711 music score titles in print as of 1981. Focus is primarily on standard repertory from the 17th through the 20th centuries, with earlier music represented by anthologies.
Level 1–3

Music Library Association, *Notes.*
"Music received" columns, issued quarterly, offer in-depth, international coverage of new scores, but with near-exclusive emphasis on western art music. An authoritative, if not highly representative selection.
Level 1–4

Winesanker, Michael, *A List of Books on Music.*
Appendices offer select lists of score anthologies (51 titles) and composers' collected editions (35 titles.)
Level 2–3

SOUND RECORDINGS
Western classical

Clough, Francis F. and G.J. Cuming, *The World's Encyclopedia of Recorded Music.* London: Sidgwick & Jackson, 1952. (Plus three supplements, published 1952–57)
Systematic listing of classical music recordings issued through 1955. Indispensable for its historical depth.
Level 4

Cohn, Arthur, *Recorded classical music: A Critical Guide to Compositions and Performances.* New York: Schirmer, 1981.
Lists close to 5,000 titles. Thorough in terms of composers and repertory. No attempt is made to sort according to more or less significant works, and there is never more than one recommended performance per piece.
Level 3–4

Gramophone. London: General Gramophone Publications, 1943-
Contains monthly column listing new classical recordings. The annual total for vol. 67 (1989–90) was about 3,500 titles.
Level 1–4

Halsey, Richard, *Classical Music Recordings for Home and Library.*
Chicago: American Library Assn., 1976.
Lists 4,101 works in 11 categories ("early" to "new and experi-
mental"). Recommended for its breadth, but its 5-point rating
system should be disregarded.
Level 1–3

Hoffmann, Frank W. *The Development of Library Collections of
Sound Recordings.* New York: Dekker, 1979.
Chapter 7 ("A basic recorded sound collection") offers a similar
but somewhat lengthier list (592 titles) than Joan Smith's "A
Basic Stock List." Largely restricted to mainstream classical and
romantic repertory.
Level 1–2

Music Library Assn., Inc., *Notes.*
Contains a quarterly index to classical (and only classical) record
reviews in a wide variety of journals. 1,964 recordings were
listed in vol. 45 (1988–1989); 3,032 in vol. 46 (1989–90).
Level 1–4

Myers, Kurtz, *Index to Record Reviews . . . between 1949 and 1977.*
Boston: G.K. Hall, 1978.

Myers, Kurtz, *Index to Record Reviews, 1978–1983.* Boston: G.K.
Hall, 1989.

Myers, Kurtz, *Index to Record Reviews, 1984–1987.* Boston: G.K.
Hall, 1989.
A cumulation of the *Notes* quarterly indexes, these publications
comprise the largest single listing of classical recordings of the
past 40 years. As an index to reviews rather than recordings, it
represents a notable type of critical synthesis and consensus.
Level 3–4

Rosenberg, Kenyon C., *A Basic Classical and Operatic Recordings Collection for Libraries*. Metuchen, N.J.: Scarecrow, 1987.

Rosenberg, Kenyon C., *A Basic Classical and Operatic Recordings Collection of Compact Discs for Libraries: A Buying Guide*. Metuchen, N.J.: Scarecrow, 1990.
Strong coverage of common-practice repertory, somewhat at the expense of early music and contemporary music. Usefully ranks pieces into three Conspectus-like tiers.
Level 1–3

Smith, Joan Pemberton, "A Basic Stock List," in Henry F.J. Currall, *Gramophone Record Libraries*. 2nd ed. London: 1970.
Core list of 400 compositions, divided evenly into primary and secondary tiers, but without recommendations as to specific recordings. Limited focus on pre-18th and 20th-century music, and a noticeable British bias.
Level 1–2

Jazz and Popular

Bruyninckx, Walter, *60 Years of Recorded Jazz: 1917–1977*. Mechelen: author, 1980– . 16 vols.

Bruyninckx, Walter, *Jazz: Modern Jazz, Be-Bop, Hard Bop, West Coast*. Mechelen: 1985– . 5 vols. to date.

Bruyninckx, Walter, *Modern Jazz: Modern Big Band*. Mechelen: 1986– .

Bruyninckx, Walter, *Progressive Jazz: Free Third Stream Fusion*. Mechelem: 1984– .
Systematic listing (approximately 150,000 titles) of jazz LPs. Cumulates and continues *Jazz Records, 1897–1942* by Rust and *Jazz Records, 1942–1969* by Jepsen.
Level 4

Cooper, B. Lee, *The Popular Music Handbook: A Resource Guide for Teachers, Librarians, and Media Specialists.* Littleton, CO: Libraries Unlimited, 1984.

Part 4 ("A basic popular music collection for libraries") lists about 750 albums. Also includes a lengthy bibliography of discographies.

Level 1–3

Harrison, Max, Charles Fox, and Eric Thatcher, *The Essential Jazz Records.* Westport: Greenwood, 1984-

Only vol. I ("Ragtime to Swing") has been published to date. Lists 250 albums with extensive commentary on each.

Level 1–3

Harrison, Max et al., *Modern Jazz; The Essential Records.* New York: Aquarius, 1975.

Five jazz critics list and evaluate 200 records from 1945–1970.

Level 1–3

Hoffman, Frank, *The Development of Library Collections of Sound Recordings.*

Sections on blues, rhythm & blues, country & western, folk, jazz, musicals/movies/radio shows, and popular (including rock) include about 480 titles in all.

Level 1–3

Hoffman, Frank and B. Lee Cooper, *The Literature of Rock II: 1979–1983.* Metuchen, N.J.: Scarecrow, 1986.

Appendix C ("A basic collection of rock recordings: 1954–1983") lists about 400 albums, divided into 24 stylistic categories.

Level 1–3

Hounsome, Terry, *Rock Record.* 3rd ed. New York: Facts on File, 1987.

Lists alphabetically over 45,000 albums by 7,678 groups or solo
artists, covering rock and related genres from their roots to the
present day.
Level 4

Jepsen, Jorgen Grunnet, *Jazz Records, 1942–1969: A Discography.*
Holte, Denmark, 1964–77.
Systematic inventory of jazz recordings. Continuation of *Jazz
Records, 1897–1942* by Rust.
Level 4

Koncandrle, Mirek, *The History of Rock and Roll: A Selective Discography.* Boston: G.K. Hall, 1988.
Over 10,000 recordings by over 1,000 artists are classified by
style and arranged chronologically, from ragtime through rap-
ping, reggae, and new age. Includes singles and LP's. Records of
special artistic or historical interest are starred.
Level 3–4

McCarthy, Albert et al., *Jazz on Record: A Critical Guide to the
First 50 Years, 1917–1967.* London: Hanover, 1968.
3,321 titles selected and annotated by four British jazz critics.
Level 3–4

Murray, James Briggs, "Understanding and Developing Black Popular Music Collections." *Drexel Library Quarterly* 19/1 (Winter,
1983), 4–54.
Provides core discography of about 130 titles, covering work
songs, spirituals, gospel, blues, rhythm & blues, soul, funk and
fusion, disco, and African-Caribbean influences. Excludes jazz.
Level 1–2

Rust, Brian, *Jazz Records, 1897–1942.* 5th ed. Chigwell: Storyville,
1982.
Comprehensive listing of 78 rpm recordings, periodically revised.
Level 4

Tarakan, Sheldon Lewis, "Classical Pop: Documenting Popular
Culture in Library Audio Collections." *Drexel Library Quarterly*,
19/1 (Winter, 1983), 123–50.
Offers core discography of about 225 titles, covering all types of
American popular music from colonial times through about 1970.
Level 1–2

Tudor, Dean, *Popular Music: An Annotated Guide to Recordings.*
Littleton, CO: Libraries Unlimited, 1983.
Wide-ranging, but selective compilation (3,070 titles). Classified
by genre into six major sections, each of which is further subdi-
vided and can be used independently in collection assessment.
Includes explanatory and critical comments.
Level 2–4

World Music

Dols, Nancy, ed., *Musics of the World: A Selective Discography.* Los
Angeles: UCLA Music Library, 1977– ; repr. 1984-
Country-by-country (or region-by-region) discography, with em-
phasis on "folk, traditional, and non-western 'classical' music."
(Introcution). Lists approximately 5 titles per locality, with high-
est recommendations first, and with annotations for each entry.
Still unique in its systematic definition of a core world music col-
lection. 339 titles in all.
Level 1–3

Ethnomusicology. Bloomington, IN: Society for Ethnomusicology,
1953-
"Currrent discography" of new commercial releases appears in
each volume. Coverage worldwide and broadly inclusive of ethnic
classical, traditional, folk, and popular musics.
Level 2–4

TECHNOLOGY FOR COLLECTION
EVALUATION: AMIGOS AND OTHER TOOLS

Sherry L. Vellucci

ABSTRACT: Technology can be used to aid in comparative collection evaluation. The OCLC Online Computer Library Center and the Amigos Bibliographic Council originally jointly developed a service for libraries to compare their machine-readable cataloging (MARC) tape records with those of other institutions. They have recently developed a microcomputer-based CD-ROM (compact disc-read only memory) product that can be used quantitatively and qualitatively to measure and analyze collections, as well as to compare one institution's collection with collections of "peer group" libraries. The OCLC/Amigos CD-ROM product is described in detail, and its applications for music libraries are reviewed and evaluated.

Of the various quantitative and qualitative techniques employed for collection evaluation, three in particular lend themselves to the application of computers to the process:

1. comparison of holdings with other institutions
2. the standard checklist method of analysis, and
3. other statistical methods of collection evaluation

It is the first method that I will spend the most time describing here: the application of technology to the comparison of your collection with those of other institutions. In fact, I was asked to examine

Sherry L. Vellucci is presently on the faculty of St. John's University, Division of Library and Information Science in Queens, New York. She was responsible for collection development and evaluation as Director of the Library at Westminster Choir College in Princeton, New Jersey.

one particular product: the *OCLC/AMIGOS Collection Analysis CD.* I was especially interested in this product because it seemed to offer an automation alternative for those of us who do not work in large research libraries. In order to provide a broader perspective on technology and collection evaluation I will also discuss briefly a few other products and automation ideas that fall into the other two categories of evaluation techniques: standard checklists and other statistical methods of collection evaluation. Before embarking on this discussion of automated collection evaluation, however, it would be appropriate to examine the technological developments, both nationally and at the OCLC Online Computer Library Center, Inc. and the AMIGOS Bibliographic Council, that led to the development of this automated product.

Background And Development

Two factors have played an important role in developing technology for collection evaluation on a national level. First is an automated library environment based on a common bibliographic communications format—the MARC (machine-readable cataloging) format. This has provided a large and ever increasing body of bibliographic data in machine-readable form as current cataloging information is added and retrospective conversion projects are undertaken and completed. Second is the development of national networks that link individual library holdings and provide access to a global library collection. The combination of these two factors has provided the right environment for the development of an automated collection development tool.[1]

The standard MARC format enables a tape-to-tape comparison of one library's holdings with another's. The AMIGOS Bibliographic Council originally used this tape comparison capability

coupled with an adapted form of the Research Libraries Group (RLG) Conspectus subject categories to provide a collection analysis service to individual "client" libraries. This service grew out of a 1984 study that analyzed the collection overlap of seventeen academic libraries participating in the Association for Higher Education of North Texas consortium.[2] Based on an earlier study at the State University of New York,[3] the participants in the Texas project had AMIGOS process their OCLC archival tapes to generate collection data for each RLG Conspectus subject category. Through this project, AMIGOS developed the software and refined the report generation process for their collection analysis service.

Influenced by the growing use and popularity of the RLG Conspectus concept of subject-based collection assessment, the system designers at OCLC wanted to develop a CD-ROM (compact disc-read only memory) prototype that complemented the Conspectus approach. Logic suggested a joint venture with the AMIGOS Bibliographic Council, which had already developed an OCLC based batch-oriented collection analysis service. Using this AMIGOS system as its basis, OCLC provided the CD-ROM development expertise, and the new *OCLC/AMIGOS Collection Analysis CD* system (*OCLC/AMIGOS*) was born.

An important result of the Texas study suggested that a broader subject classification breakdown was more relevant to a wider range of libraries outside the large Association of Research Libraries (ARL) institutions.[4] Thus, the *OCLC/AMIGOS* system-development team substituted the National Shelf-List 500 Count (NSL) for the RLG Conspectus as the basis for subject categories. Also based on the Library of Congress *Classification* scheme (LCC), the NSL divides the classification broadly into 500 categories, or ranges. Table 1 contains a comparison between the NSL and the RLG Conspectus for the LCC M1-M1490 range.

In developing a complementary product, the OCLC system designers identified four major differences between the *OCLC/AMI-*

APPENDIX A
COMPARISON OF NATIONAL SHELF LIST 500 COUNT
and RLG CONSPECTUS
MUSIC SECTION M1-M1490

RLG Conspectus	*NSL 500 COUNT*
General Music	
MUS1 - Collections = M1	M1-M0004 - Music Collections;
Manuscripts	
MUS2 - Music printed or copied in ms.	
in U.S. before 1860 =	M1.A1.-.A15
MUS3 - Collections of musical sources =	M2
MUS4 - Collected works of individual	
composers =	M3-3.1
MUS5 - First editions =	M3.3
Instrumental Music	
MUS6 - Collections of instrumental	M0005-M1490 - Instrumental
music =	M5 music
MUS7 - Organ music =	M6-19
MUS8 - Piano music =	M20-39
MUS9 - Music for other solo instruments =	M40-175
MUS10 - Instrumental music for motion	
pictures, radio, T.V. =	M176
MUS11 - Collections of music, 2 or more	
solo instruments =	M177-179
MUS12 - Duets: organ/harmonium =	M180-195
MUS13 - Piano, for 3,4,5,6,7, etc. hands,	
two pianos =	M200-216
MUS14 - Piano and 1 other instrument =	M217-285
MUS15 - Duets without keyboard	
instruments =	M286-298
MUS16 - Chamber ensembles: trios -	
nonets and larger combinations of	
purely chamber music =	M300-986
MUS17 - Chamber music for early	
instruments =	M990
MUS18 - Orchestral music: symphonies,	
concertos, etc. =	M1000-1075
MUS19 - String orchestra music:	
symphonies, concertos =	M1100-1160
MUS20 - Band music =	M1200-1270
MUS21 - Music for reduced orchestra,	
dance orchestra, jazz, other special	
ensembles =	M1350-1366
MUS22 - Instrumental music for	
children =	M1375-1420
MUS23 - Dance music =	M1450
MUS24 - Chance compositions, electronic	
music, music with color apparatus, etc. =	M1470-1480
MUS25 - Music before 1700 =	M1490

GOS and RLG Conspectus approaches to collection assessment. According to Martin Dillon and others at OCLC:

1. the Conspectus is subjective and qualitative; the prototype is objective and quantitative;
2. the Conspectus categories are applied to shelf list counts in the aggregate; the prototype is based on titles;
3. the Conspectus requires intensive manual labor, both in its original assessments, and even more so if the assessments are to be validated by shelf counts; the prototype is fully automated; and,
4. the Conspectus emphasizes resource sharing; the prototype is designed to facilitate collection assessment.[5]

In addition, the designers of the *OCLC/AMIGOS* system identified eight objectives for a stand-alone system that would allow a library to compare its collection with other collections. These objectives were:

1. to enable direct collection budgeting across all major subject areas of a collection;
2. to aid departmental budgeting;
3. to assist in the selection of individual titles for acquisition;
4. to assist librarians working with scholars and faculty members in the evaluation of a collection in their areas of expertise;
5. to assist the accrediting process by allowing comparisons with a group of peer libraries;
6. to project cost of acquisitions for a new program;
7. to evaluate collection development policies; and,
8. to assist in the cooperative development of collections among a group of libraries.[6]

The designers proceeded with the basic premise that in order to achieve these goals the system must provide large amounts of data, include sophisticated collection metrics with immediate response time, have a user friendly interface, and extract data easily. These objectives were achieved in part by providing collection metrics data that had been precalculated on a mainframe computer prior to inclusion on the CD-ROM disk, thus giving the impression of instant calculations for any statistical information requested.

Computer generated and analyzed collection data can be a powerful resource for any collection manager. According to Ann Armbrister, formerly of AMIGOS:

> Such analysis constitutes an important validity check, allowing collection development staff to assess the yield of their policies in numbers of titles added to targeted areas of library collections. As these . . . information resources come to be more fully utilized, they have the potential of transforming the decision-making process in libraries.[7]

In light of this potential, I would like to offer a few general caveats about computer-based evaluation methods.

First, in any quantitative measure of a collection's worth, be cautious and critical of the data and methods used. Second, be cautious about drawing conclusions from partial data; be sure you know what is included in and what is missing from the data you are analyzing or comparing. Third, be sure you are comparing apples with apples. There are few valid reasons for comparing the collections of institutions that have different objectives, programs and user populations. And finally, beware of any analysis that lacks some type of **qualitative** measure. Certainly use any valid quantitative methods available to you when they are appropriate, but don't use them as your sole measure. Never overlook the qualitative factors that are important in the relationship between your library's collection and your particular users' needs.[8] After pronouncing these caveats, it is time to examine the *OCLC/AMIGOS*

Collection Analysis CD system and its potential use in music libraries.

What Is It?

OCLC/AMIGOS is a stand-alone microcomputer based system that enables you to perform various types of collection evaluation. You can:

1. quantitatively and qualitatively measure and analyze your own collection, and
2. quantitatively and qualitatively compare your collection with the collections of peer group libraries.

For my analysis of the product, I used a Demonstration program of version 1.3 provided by AMIGOS, that contained 1.6 million records in all subject areas for items published during the 10 year period 1977–1987. (The current software is version 2.01, contains 1.7 million records, and includes the 10 year period 1980–1990.)

TECHNICAL SPECIFICATIONS

The *OCLC/AMIGOS Collection Analysis CD* system has the following basic requirements for operation:

1. a Microcomputer, either an OCLC M310 or later model Workstation, or an IBM-PC AT or compatible;
2. a 20-40 MB hard-disk drive or larger, depending on number of user-defined peer groups;
3. A high-density 5-1/4 inch floppy disk drive;
4. one compact disk (CD) drive (they recommend Hitachi);

5. an IBM Disk Operating System (DOS) version 3.1 or higher;

6. MS-DOS CD-ROM extensions 2.00 or greater, and

7. A printer is optional

When you purchase the CD system you receive:

1. a compact disk that contains the aggregated peer group data extracted from the OCLC database and approximately 1.7 million abbreviated bibliographic records for titles published within a recent 10 year period;

2. your own library's data on several high density diskettes for the same 10 year period, and,

3. system software on one high density diskette.

A user's manual accompanies the package. After the initial purchase, an annual subscription updates the disks on a yearly basis, to include the latest ten years worth of bibliographic records and collection data.

OCLC/AMIGOS offers two package options for peer group definition. The Standard Program comes with fourteen pre-set academic peer groups, defined according to collection size and degree programs supported (see appendix B). The Standard Plus Program option includes the same fourteen pre-set peer groups as the Standard package, but allows you to define up to four additional peer groups customized specifically for your library's data comparison needs. For example, a conservatory library could define its customized peer group to include only data from other conservatory libraries.

The Bibliographic Records included in the database are defined by the following criteria:

APPENDIX B

PEER GROUP INDEX

	Peer Group Name (Members)	Titles	Holdings
1	ARL Libraries in OCLC (77)	1424644	14885203
2	ARL 1st Quartile (Largest) (14)	1167641	4545167
3	ARL 2nd Quartile (Next Largest) (27)	928879	5077417
4	Select Academic Libraries (66)	732470	6717283
5	Academic Libraries > 700,000 (59)	704292	6196275
6	Select Academics - High Admission Stds (27)	512074	2425814
7	Academic Libraries 300-699,999 (140)	698721	9271872
8	Academics 300-699,999 with Doctrl Pgms (47)	513912	3276504
9	Academics 300-699,999 with Bach & Mstrs (89)	588085	5796056
10	Academics 100-299,999 (367)	649349	10625827
11	Academics 100-299,999 with grad degrees (243	594260	7606539
12	Academics 100-299,999 four year degrees (109	387549	2674058
13	Academics 50,000-100,000 (173)	400431	2230167
14	The Database (990)	1650091	48162487

ENTER (Select/Exit)   Up Arrow   Down Arrow

1. they must be non-serial printed materials;
2. they must have a Library of Congress *Classification* number present; and,
3. they must be held by at least one Association of Research Libraries member library or academic library

These criteria present some obvious problems for music libraries, that will be addressed later in this paper.

What Does It Do?

The system generates statistical reports and bibliographic lists that provide a broad overview of your collection as well as detailed title-by-title comparisons based on the Library of Congress Classification schedule.[9] It performs overlap analysis, reveals

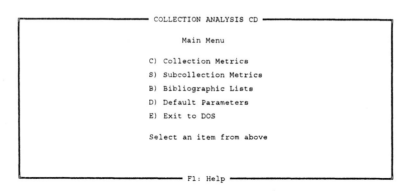

```
 ──────────── COLLECTION ANALYSIS CD ────────────
│                                                 │
│                    Main Menu                    │
│                                                 │
│         C)  Collection Metrics                  │
│         S)  Subcollection Metrics               │
│         B)  Bibliographic Lists                 │
│         D)  Default Parameters                  │
│         E)  Exit to DOS                         │
│                                                 │
│         Select an item from above               │
│                                                 │
│                                                 │
 ──────────────── F1: Help ───────────────────────
```

Figure 1. Main Menu.

widely or scarcely held items, identifies gaps in your collection, or unique items in your own or peer group collections. By altering the analysis parameters you can analyze the impact of various acquisition strategies and produce customized bibliographies. *OCLC/AMIGOS* is menu driven and easy to use.

When you first log-on to the system you are presented with the Main Menu (figure 1), which offers a variety of system activities. You can select to extract broad collection or subcollection metrics, create bibliographic lists or set default parameters.

QUANTITATIVE ANALYSIS

The system is designed as a two-step process. The first step is a quantitative analysis. Here *OCLC/AMIGOS* allows you to perform six different statistical analyses of your collection at either the broad collection-level (32 ranges) or the narrower subcollection-level (500 ranges). As seen in figure 2, the report options include counts, proportions, overlap, holdings distribution, gap and uniqueness. These analyses are intended to identify the strengths and weaknesses of your collection as compared to peer group collections. Based upon this statistical information, collection development

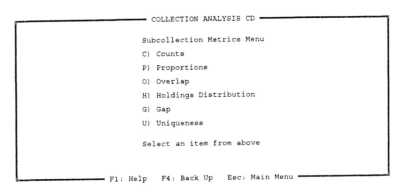

Figure 2. Subcollection Metrics Menu.

librarians can make decisions regarding acquisition priorities and budgeting. Although broader level analysis is possible, I have limited my examples to the subcollection-level, where examination can focus on a music collection. At this level the LCC classes are broken down according to ranges defined by the National Shelf List 500 count. I have selected only two of these reports to examine in this paper: proportions and gaps.

The subcollection proportions report (figure 3) gives simple percentages that compare the size of your collection in the designated range of the NSL classes with that of the selected peer group and an average member of the peer group. The report gives you information on the number of titles held in your collection; the number of titles held by the "average member" (determined by the formula: no. of peer group titles, divided by the no. of peer group members); the comparative size of your collection compared with the average member collection (determined by the formula: no. of your titles, divided by the no. of average member titles); the percentage of the peer group's collection represented by this portion of the class range (determined by the formula: no. of peer group titles in range, e.g., MT1-MT9999, divided by the total peer group titles

Subcollection Proportions M-MZ Music
Peer Group: Academic Libraries > 700,000 (59)

NSL 500	------ Titles ------		Comparative Size	- Pct of Subcollection -	
	Evaluator	Avg Mbr		Peer Group	Evaluator
M1-M0004	2	2	1.00	0.1	0.1
M0005-M1490	0	0	0.00	0.0	0.0
M1495-M5000	2	2	1.00	0.1	0.1
ML-ML9999	2,377	1,484	1.60	84.6	84.1
MT1-MT9999	447	266	1.68	15.2	15.8
TOTALS	2,828	1,754	1.61	100.00	100.00

Figure 3. Subcollection Proportions: M-MZ Music.

in LCC class, e.g., M-MZ); and, the percentage of your collection
represented by each portion of the class range. In figure 3 for example, 15.2% of the peer group's total holdings in the M class are
represented by MT's, while 15.8% of the evaluator's collection is
comprised of MT's. This would indicate that proportionally your
collection approximates that of the peer group in this range. It also
gives you an idea of the proportional breakdown of your collection
by class ranges.

The subcollection gap report (figure 4) shows the size of your
holdings compared with the selected peer group. This may reveal
gaps in your collection and shows the effects of various acquisition
strategies if you decided to fill specific gaps. For example, figure 4
shows that the evaluator library is missing very few titles that are
held by most peer group libraries in the ranges 80–89% and
90–100%, thus indicating a strong core collection in this area. Also
note that the evaluator library is missing 47 titles that are held by
50–59% of the libraries in the peer group comparison (29–34 of the
59 libraries in the peer group). The evaluating library could use
this information to strengthen the collection in this range. In the
last column, comparative size, the percentage expresses the size of
your collection compared with the average peer library as a result
of purchasing all gap titles up to and including that particular
range (73 titles). These purchases, therefore, would put your library

Subcollection Gap
Peer Group: Academic Libraries > 700,000 (59)

Division		Holdings Range	Gap Titles In Range	Gap Titles Cumulative	Comparative Size
ML-ML9999		90-100%	1	1	160%
Literature of Music		80-89%	0	1	160%
		70-79%	6	7	161%
Current:		60-69%	19	26	161%
Evaluator Titles	2,377	50-59%	47	73	163%
Comparative Size	160%	40-49%	94	167	167%
		30-39%	157	324	171%
		20-29%	315	639	181%
		10-19%	827	1,466	216%
		1-09%	2,625	4,091	337%
		Unique	2,775	6,866	347%
TOTAL		0-100%	6,866	6,866	347%

Figure 4. Subcollection Gaps.

at 163% of the average peer library, while your current comparative size is 160%, as seen from the information given in the far left column. This report is based on a "most-held-first" acquisition strategy that supports the idea that titles held by the greatest number of peers are the most desirable. On the other hand, since the comparative size of your library is already considerably larger than the average peer (60% larger), you may decide to adjust your acquisitions strategy to purchase materials that would strengthen another area of your collection. In either event, it is the second facet of *OCLC/AMIGOS* that allows you to identify the specific titles in a given range.

QUALITATIVE ANALYSIS

The second step in using *OCLC/AMIGOS* involves qualitative selection. The system can provide a list of items held by the peer group but not by the evaluator library. Using this bibliographic information, the collection development librarian must apply qualitative judgement in selecting items in accordance with the established acquisition priorities of the library. The bibliographic lists function is used for this part of the process. It is here that the beginning and ending LCC class parameters can be narrowed to a single class number for very detailed comparisons.

The bibliographic lists menu (figure 5) offers six categories of analysis that are slightly different from those offered by the metric reports menus. These include overlap, gap, unique evaluator, unique peer group, evaluator list and peer group list. In all of the bibliographic lists functions, the output is in the form of bibliographic record citations, rather than numeric data. To illustrate simply some of these functions, imagine the following scenario: your music education department has decided to begin a program in oboe methods, and wants to know whether your library has the latest material in this area.

The analysis process begins by setting the parameters for the search. As the parameter screen in figure 6 shows, I have selected peer group 5, academic libraries set 700,000 volumes; I've set both the beginning and ending LCC class numbers at MT360 so that the analysis will include only that class number; I've set the holdings parameters to 100% in order to see items in all holdings ranges; I've asked to search the full 10 years of the database, and I've requested items in all languages.

Examining the results of one analysis of your MT360 collection, we see that the evaluator titles list (Figure 7) for this class number showed that you had only one item in your MT360 collection that fell within this set of parameters. The bibliographic list provides truncated author/title information, the year of publication, the selected class number, and the total number of titles held by the evaluator in that class range.

The peer group titles report (figure 8) provides a listing of all titles held within the peer group. The asterisk denotes a title that is held by the evaluator library. From the holdings information in the far right column, we can see that the item held by our

```
──────────────── COLLECTION ANALYSIS CD ────────────────

            Bibliographic Lists Menu

            O)  Overlap

            G)  Gap

            U)  Unique Evaluator

            N)  Unique Peer Group

            E)  Evaluator List

            P)  Peer Group List

            Select an item from above


──────── F1: Help    F4: Back Up    Esc: Main Menu ────────
```

Figure 5. Bibliographic Lists Menu.

```
──────── Gap Between Evaluator and Peer Group ────────
       Peer Group: 5          Academic Libraries > 700,000

 LC Class Beginning: MT360
            Ending: MT360     This LC Class range contains 7 record(s)

 Holdings Pct Lower:   0
             Upper: 100       Items held by 0 - 100% of the peer group

 Pub. Year Beginning: 1978
             Ending: 1988     Publication years 1978 to 1988

           Language: ALL      All Languages

      Output Device: S        Enter S for Screen, P for Printer

     Save File Name: A:\AMIGOS2.DAT


──────── F1: Help    F4: Back Up    F8: Initiate    Esc: Main Menu ────────
```

Figure 6. Parameter Screen: Gap Between Evaluator and Peer
*   Group*

library is held by a total of 20 libraries in the peer group. If holding
frequency is a measure of quality, which is the assumption upon
which the most-held-first acquisition policy is based, then this must
be an important title in the MT360 class.

Since there are so few titles retrieved in this search, it is
easy to ascertain that there are four items listed here that are not
held in our own collection. If the search had produced a lengthy

```
                        Evaluator Titles
              XYZ       Pub Year: 1978-88     Lang: ALL


  LC Class    Author / Title                                  Pub Yr
 ──────────────────────────────────────────────────────────────────
  1 MT360     Rothwell, Evelyn. / Oboe technique    Evelyn R    1982
              Total records in this range = 1
```

Figure 7. Evaluator Titles.

```
                         Peer Group Titles
               XYZ to Academic Libraries > 700,000 (59)
     Holdings Range: 0-100% (1-59 libraries)   Pub Year: 1978-88  Lang: ALL


     LC Class    Author / Title                     Pub Yr  Peer Holds
    ──────────────────────────────────────────────────────────────────
     1 MT360     Goossens, Leon, 1897 / Oboe   Leon Goossens a  1980      3
     2 MT360     Paulu, Catherine. / Let's play oboe   by Cath  1986      2
     3 MT360     Prodan, James C. / Oboe performance practices 1979      8
     4 MT360     Prodan, James C. / Oboe performance practices 1979      1
     5 MT360   * Rothwell, Evelyn. / Oboe technique   Evelyn R 1982     20
                Total records in this range = 5
```

Figure 8. Peer Group Titles.

list, as a search in many of the ML categories would have done, we could have ascertained easily the lacunae in our collection by performing a gap search. This would have extracted only those titles not held by the evaluator library.

Any title listed can be called up for a fuller bibliographic display (figure 9), which provides abbreviated information extracted from the OCLC bibliographic record. This information includes author, title, publisher, year of publication, ISBN (when present) and the OCLC control number. In this display, the author information is limited to 20 characters, and the title field is limited to 80 characters. These abbreviated bibliographic records are designed to give enough bibliographic information so that the full bibliographic records can be located in the OCLC Online Union Catalog (OLUC).

These records can also be saved to a disk for further manipulation. Figure 10 shows the abbreviated records as they appear in the saved file.

```
─────────────── Full Bibliographic Display ───────────────
Prodan, James C.
  Oboe performance practices and teaching in the United States and
  Canada   compile
Institute for Woodwind Research,    1979
OCLC = 5069771

Press any key to continue...
```

Figure 9. Full Bibliographic Display.

BIBLIOGRAPHIC RECORDS SAVED TO A FILE

Goossens, Leon, 1897
Oboe Leon Goossens and Edwin Roxburgh.
Macdonald, 1980
OCLC =   7565964
ISBN = 354045954

Paulu, Catherine.
Let's play oboe by Catherine Paulu.
Fox Products Corp., 1986
OCLC = 14868241
ISBN =   0

Prodan, James C.
Oboe performance practices and teaching in the United States and
Canada compile
Institute for Woodwind Research, 1979
OCLC = 5069771
ISBN =   0

Prodan, James C.
Oboe performance practices and teaching in the United States and
Canada compile
Spectrum Music Publishers, 1979
OCLC = 11478191
ISBN =   0

Figure 10. Bibliographic Records in a Save File.

This overview of *OCLC/AMIGOS* functions was designed to give some idea of the potential usefulness of this CD-ROM system. It is indeed user friendly and produces clear and concise statistical and bibliographic reports. In spite of this, however, there are several problems that seriously affect the usefulness of this system for music libraries.

First is the time-frame limitation on the database. For the sciences, holdings representing the most recent 10 years of publications are probably an accurate measure of a collection's worth, since the literature of the sciences is cumulative, incorporative, collective and consensual, with the ideas of the past embodied in the literature of the present. The literature of the humanities, however, is noncumulative and nonconsensual, requiring researchers to refer to works that have appeared throughout the entire time breadth of the discipline.[10] How can we determine the adequacy of our collections based only upon information for titles published within the last 10 years? Certainly from this we can tell whether we have missed any important recent publications, but that is all. The restrictive time frame, however, is not the only reason for the appearance of so few music scores in the demonstration database. There is a second serious drawback for music users that I found when I searched the (OLUC) for the full bibliographic records of the two scores that existed in the evaluator collection of my demo version. I discovered that both of the bibliographic records for these music scores had been classed correctly, but had been entered in the OCLC books format, as had many of the other records for items in the M class ranges for music scores in the *OCLC/AMIGOS* database. One problem, therefore, lies with the original cataloging for those records in the OLUC. These bibliographic records were either entered in the wrong format, or were incorrectly classed. This supports my assertion that any automated system such as this is only as good as the database, and hence the cataloging, upon which it is based.

So, it appears that only printed items in the books format file of the OLUC are included in the *OCLC/AMIGOS* database. Thus, while the system could prove useful for assessing the music literature portion of a music collection, it cannot assist in evaluating those portions of a collection that include periodicals, scores, sound recordings, video recordings and other media materials. Other shortcomings with this system for use with a music collection pale by comparison, so I will only mention them briefly.

First, the evaluator collection and all peer group records must be classed in the Library of Congress *Classification*, and the class number must be present on the OCLC master record (information is not drawn from peer group archival tapes). This might be expanded to include the *Dewey Decimal Classification* in the future, but not other classification systems such as Dickinson, nor is there any means to convert these variant class numbers at this time for this CD-ROM product.

Second, although useful for a broad overview with a general collection, the use of the broad ranges defined by the National Shelf List (i.e., M1-M4; M5-M1494; M1495-M5000; ML1-ML9999; MT1-MT9999) are less than ideal for a detailed statistical evaluation of a music collection. The greater detail provided by the RLG Conspectus subject ranges is better suited for assessing a special subject collection such as music. And finally, uneven database coverage caused by libraries in various stages of retrospective conversion projects can present skewed information. To give *OCLC/AMIGOS* its due, this was the original reason behind restricting the database to the most current 10 years.

Obviously, in light of these shortcomings, it appears that we will have to wait a while longer for a stand-alone CD-ROM system for collection evaluation that meets the needs of music libraries. This is unfortunate, for this CD-ROM product could have been especially useful for non-academic libraries by selecting the option of a client-defined peer group.

Other Automated Evaluation Methods

Now let's examine briefly some alternative automated approaches to collection evaluation. In addition to the CD-ROM product, AMIGOS offers a collection analysis custom tape match for a single library or a consortium of libraries. AMIGOS will run your archival tape on their mainframe collection analysis system, comparing it to any single library or group of libraries that you request, providing permission is granted by the "compared" library. Subject categories for this custom tape match can be based on the RLG Conspectus, the Pacific Northwest Group's Conspectus or other machine-readable classification tables. Nine standard or any customized reports are available. If you only need a one-time analysis of your collection, this could be a viable alternative for you to consider. This method would be useful for public libraries as well as academic.

Another service offered by several vendors including AMIGOS, WLN and Brodart, is the "BCL3" tape match. This is the application of technology to the standard checklist method of collection evaluation, where you compare your collection against a recognized standard list, rather than basing the comparison on frequency counts. The vendor will run your archival tape against a tape version of the third edition of *Books for College Libraries*, using an author/title match, and will produce a machine-readable or printed report on any gaps in your collection. Most vendors will not run subclasses separately, i.e., just the music portion of a collection, so this analysis is something you would have to participate in as part of a library-wide project. This again would be a one-time analysis of your collection, one that several libraries have found useful as part of the self-evaluation study for accreditation review purposes.

If your institution has the computing power and expertise, *Books for College Libraries* is available for direct purchase in magnetic tape form from the Association of College & Research Libraries. The tape provides raw data only; your own institution would have to mount the tape on your mainframe and provide the software to match records with those on your archival tape or in your online catalog.[11]

Finally, I would like to mention one other automated approach to collection evaluation that is currently used in several academic libraries, and is possible to perform on a microcomputer with a good database program. This is a statistical evaluation based upon course analysis.[12] This method assumes that a valid measure of a collection's worth is its ability to support the curriculum.

Library of Congress *Classification* numbers (or any classification schedule), and *Library of Congress Subject Headings* are assigned to each course in the curriculum, based upon course content as described in the college catalog, course syllabus, assigned reading lists and comments of the teachers. More than one class number or range can be assigned to each course. Additional information can be added to the database including department codes (to identify interdepartmental collection use), course levels (to assist in determining necessary collection depth for a given classification range), and number of students enrolled in the course. The information can then be sorted by class number, subject headings, individual courses, or departments. Information on the library's holdings in each class range can then be compared to identify course use in specific ranges, in order to determine the adequacy of the collection to support curricular needs. Having the ability to analyze this information at your fingertips can prove useful in setting collection development priorities, establishing budgetary needs, and providing faculty and administration with a profile of collection use and library strengths and weaknesses in relation to the curriculum.

Summary

Where does this leave us in our quest for automating the labor intensive process of collection evaluation? What my investigation implies is that the less expensive, totally automated systems designed for inhouse use such as *OCLC/AMIGOS*, are a great idea with serious flaws for smaller, highly specialized collections such as music. The customized tape matching methods would prove either too expensive for most music libraries, or would require that we participate as part of a larger, library-wide collection analysis, something over which we do not usually have control. The microcomputer technology application, currently most useful for an academic music library, is also the most labor intensive in that much time must be spent collecting data, assigning class numbers and subject headings, and developing the program.

Obviously, we are only just beginning to realize the benefits of automation in this area; but we should not abandon hope. The music library community has proved effective in its past lobbying efforts, and perhaps it can convince corporations like OCLC, AMIGOS and WLN that music libraries are a viable market for their products, if they meet our specialized needs. To support our demands, further research is needed: studies are required that examine the proportion of bibliographic records in the OCLC music scores format that include Library of Congress and Dewey class numbers; bibliometric studies are needed on the aging and rates of obsolescence of music literature; classification tables need to be developed that enable conversion from one classification scheme to another; studies are needed that investigate ways to include nonprint and unclassed materials in automated collection evaluation systems. We should encourage OCLC and its members to continue to clean up the bibliographic database. And undergirding all of this, we must educate the best possible music catalogers, in the understanding that technology has given us the means to utilize the end products of their work in more ways than were dreamt of in their philosophy.

Notes And References

1. For further discussion see Ann Armbrister, "Library MARC Tapes as a Resource for Collection Analysis: The AMIGOS Service," *Advances in Library Automation and Networking* 2 (1988): 120.

2. Thomas E. Nisonger, "Editing the RLG Conspectus to Analyze the OCLC Archival Tapes of Seventeen Texas Libraries," *Library Resources & Technical Services* 29 (1985): 309-27.

3. Glyn T. Evans, Roger Gifford, and Donald R. Franz, *Collection Development Analysis Using OCLC Archival Tapes: Final Report*, ERIC Document ED 152 299 (Albany, N.Y.: SUNY Office of Library Services, 1977).

4. Nisonger, "Editing the RLG Conspectus," p. 323-4.

5. Martin Dillon, Dave Stephens, Kevin Flash and Mark Crook, "Design Issues for a Microcomputer-Based Collection Analysis System," *Microcomputers for Information Management* 10, no. 5 (1984): 265.

6. Dillon et al, "Design issues," p. 263-4.

7. Armbrister, "Library MARC Tapes," p. 123.

8. G. Edward Evans, *Developing Library and Information Center Collections* (Littleton, Colo.: Libraries Unlimited, 1987), p. 320.

9. *OCLC/AMIGOS Collection Analysis CD: User Guide* (Dublin, Ohio: OCLC Online Computer Library Center, 1989), p. 1.1.

10. Sherry L. Vellucci, "Uniform Titles as Linking Devices," *Cataloging & Classification Quarterly* 12, no. 1 (1990): 46.

11. For an example of one library's approach to this see Michael Kreyche, "BCL3 and NOTIS: An Automated Collection Analysis Project," *Library Acquisitions: Practice & Theory* 13, no. 4 (1989): 323-8.

12. For examples of this evaluation method see Michael R. Gabriel, "Online Collection Evaluation, Course by Course," *Collection Building* 8, no. 2 (1987): 20-24; Elliot Palais, "Use of Course Analysis in Compiling a Collection Development Policy Statement for a University Library," *Journal of Academic Librarianship* 13 (1987): 8-13.

Evaluating the Conspectus Approach:
Problems and Alternatives

Lenore Coral

ABSTRACT: The Conspectus approach to collection assessment does
not necessarily aid librarians in understanding their collection's specific holdings or defining their collecting policies. Its results are also
too subjective to allow for meaningful comparison of collections between institutions. If we want a tool to compare collections then we
must develop a tool for analysis that more closely reveals the choices
that govern collection development in music.

When in the course of library events it becomes necessary to do
collection-assessment, how should it be done? What are the means
available to us and what are the limitations imposed by these
schemes? If the prevailing systems are found deficient what can we
substitute for them?

First, I think that we have to ask what the purpose of this
assessment is. What is the goal we are trying to achieve? Are we
trying to define our collecting policy within the institution that the
collection serves? Or are we trying to compare our own collection to
other collections? These two goals are in fact very different, and the
means to achieve them, I believe, ought to be different. Some of the
options in vogue today do not seem to differentiate between these
goals.

Others writing for this volume have articulated their belief
in the efficacy of the analysis of a collection provided by the "Conspectus." This tool, developed by the RLG Collection Management
and Development Committee, was designed in its beginning as a
tool for comparing the strengths of the collections in member libraries of the Research Libraries Group. Although this group (RLG)

thought of itself as quite homogeneous, the relative strengths of the constituent parts of its members do vary enormously, so that what were being compared were not always similar collections from similar sorts of programs or institutions.

I admit that I have very little use for the Conspectus. I do not believe that it achieves our goals, nor do I believe that it can serve any meaningful function. Why such a strong statement? Twice in my career I have moved to new positions, this after having begun my professional career in a brand new library. How did I go about establishing what the collection I had become responsible for contained, where its strengths were, and what I should be collecting to enhance it? Well, I did essentially the same thing both times, even though when I arrived at the second institution, Cornell, the Music Conspectus had been completed. I studied the collection in the stacks. I marked catalogs and checked them against the library catalog. Nothing in the Conspectus helped me to understand the Cornell collection in a way different from the procedures I had to use at the University of Wisconsin without the Conspectus. Let me give you one example. Cornell has a collection rich in opera. It is listed as a level 4 in the Conspectus. That 4 gave me no clues that the strengths of the collection are in its 19th-century French opera scores and its rich collection of Alessandro Scarlatti sources. It did not reveal the collection of Rameau operas or the Lully scores in our collection. Nor did it tell me that Cornell's collection was not strong in the operas of 19th-century Italy, other than those of the major composers. If it did not tell me much about what I could expect to find it certainly did not tell me how the Cornell collection compares with those of other institutions also claiming 4s in this category. The recently completed retrospective conversion project for this segment of the collection (Cornell is among the last of the Associated Music Libraries Group libraries to convert this segment of its collection)[1] has revealed a hit rate of only 64%. This more clearly reveals the strength of this segment of our collection and seems to provide more useful comparative data than the Conspectus numbers.

As has been described, participants in the Conspectus project assign parallel numbers from 0 to 5 which are meant to indicate existing collection strength and current collecting intensity. These numeric values are assigned to predetermined subsets of the Library of Congress *Classification* (LCC) code. The subsets themselves will be discussed later in this paper. The resulting tables represent a pseudo-scientific analysis of a collection. The process of assigning the numbers is based on a gut reaction to the collection and a belief on the part of the participant in the current level of collecting, but the results mask this unscientific method in the aura of numeracy. They do not really reveal ways in which a collection is strong, or where it is weak.

What are the kinds of decisions we make in developing a collection development policy for an institution? Or, what are the factors that inform decisions? I know of no institution today that is financially able to buy everything (even if they would want to), nor one that was able to collect everything in the past, so how do we describe our choices? I think that we could make a list: by chronological periods, geographical factors, lists of individual authors or composers, intellectual level of the material, quality or aims of the edition, and categories of subject matter and genre, which in academic institutions are usually tied to the curriculum and the research program. With the sole exception of the categories of genre and subject, none of these criteria are reflected in the LCC scheme for music. I hasten to add that this and further comments are not meant to be construed as criticisms of that classification scheme, but only of the meanings we have hung on it in the course of this futile exercise.

If the goal of the Conspectus project is to allow comparison of collections then it has failed. For its results are too subjective and too unspecific to allow for these comparisons. They are subjective in the very act of each individual interpreting definitions such as that for level 4: "Major published sources required for dissertations and independent research. What is meant by 'major' and how does it link to 'research,' which often enough requires access to the apparently 'minor'? Would the definition of research not vary widely from institution to institution depending on the type of work being carried on in each? How then can level 4s assigned in different institutions be comparable? Or for level 5, which states that a "comprehensive" collection is one in which a library "endeavors so far as is reasonably possible, to include all significant works of recorded knowledge . . . in all applicable languages, for a necessarily defined and limited field? The qualification of every noun by its host of attendant adjectives begs the question of compatibility of analysis from one selector to the next. How does one go about deciding what level of collection or collecting in any subject matches that of the Conspectus? Do we not feel some uneasiness at the attaching of numbers to such a process? Or are these numbers used in a self-serving way, so that the former glory of a collection is reflected in a high number for the past but (in a perhaps cynical attempt to garner additional funding in a time of tight money) a lower number is ascribed for the current collecting level. If we cannot describe in words what we are doing, how can we describe this complex process in terms of numbers? Do we go back and revise the Conspectus as fashions in scholarship change? Probably not, since the classification scheme is too ossified to reflect these changes and the Conspectus classes too broad for it to matter.

Certainly, a good bit of the rhetoric attached to this project has dealt with attempts to define meaningful ways to verify the assignment of these numbers. There are two methods that I am aware of. One is to select a sample of the literature listed in some published bibliographies. This sampling is then tested against each of the collections. The results that I have seen from such studies do not seem to corroborate the results of this test with the numbers in the Conspectus. Jeffry Larson, the author of the French language and literature Conspectus verification study, proposed that we understand the results in comparison with the group tested—in other words, grading on the curve instead of in absolute terms.[2] Such a method of interpretation allows for self-fulfilling results. The other scheme is to revitalize the shelflist measurement project. True, there are many flaws with this seemingly empirical device: different uses of the classification scheme, problems resulting from a variety of styles for analytical entries and for what is filed into a shelflist that skew the results, and the crude fact that no collection is complete and that all that is measured in this kind of study is quantity, not quality. Still, this method is more revealing, I believe, than the self-definitional process of the Conspectus as a device for comparison. It offers real (if suspect) data. But comparisons between institutions need to be thoughtfully controlled.

It has often been stated in the literature of collection development that institutions offering similar graduate programs will need to have a core collection of printed materials in their libraries if these programs are to succeed. I would assert that this is indeed true of academic music libraries. It would be interesting to do a study of the holdings of the 7 participating AMLG libraries once the score retrospective conversion projects are completed. It continues to surprise me as the tail-end Charlie of this project that the Cornell hit-rate (that is, the rate of finding machine-readable records) in such well collected classes as M2 was no higher than 68%.

What is it we want to describe in enunciating a collection policy? Not, surely, that one collects or does not collect materials according to the Library of Congress scheme for arranging them on the shelf. Rather, what periods do we emphasize? What kind of editions do we select? That is, once the core repertory is there what causes us to buy another edition? How do we select the composers that we buy? Are there particular segments of the repertory that we ignore or select very lightly in? Do we buy arrangements or didactic editions? The problem with the RLG Music Conspectus is that virtually none of these decisions are revealed in it. The LC classification scheme for music does not provide the kind of detail or organization that describes our collecting activities. Saying that you collect at a certain level in a particular genre does not clarify either whose works you collect nor what kinds of editions you collect. Those are, for me at least, the interesting questions.

The Conspectus groups numbers from the classification scheme into groups or subsets. These subsets do not always make particularly coherent or sensible groupings of classes from the selector's point of view. Look, for example, at Conspectus groups MUS27 (LC classes M1500-1526: operas, incidental music, and ballets) and MUS16 (M300-986: all chamber ensembles larger than duets). Think for a moment about what it would mean to see a high number in MUS27. Does the reporting library really collect equally in the genres of opera, intermezzi, and ballets, or does this number really reflect only a strong opera collection? Analogous questions arise when pondering a high number in MUS16. A closer look at the way the Conspectus has divided the classification scheme has led me to believe that its developers have privileged the classes not normally collected in depth in research institutions, perhaps to meet their goal of discovering who was covering these less frequently collected materials, while lumping into large groups those classes we normally expect to find well covered in constituent RLG libraries. These groupings, while serving one of their aims—that of assigning collection responsibility for materials infrequently collected in research libraries—will not yield satisfactory descriptions of our normal collecting activities. Isn't that what we really want to describe? Within each of our collections we collect more heavily in some genres than in others. How can we show this relativity within the constraints of the Conspectus groupings? And, finally, how does our collecting activity compare to the total worldwide output? Moreover, do we really care about the latter question?

I guess that what I am trying to say is that it is extremely difficult to compare collections in this abstract kind of way. Each of us charged with selection can describe what we believe we are doing within our collection. I think that we should then let the databases speak for our collections. In general the user is not interested in an abstract idea—that is, which collection is strong in what. That person wants to know who owns specific titles and editions, or, at least, is a collection strong in a particular genre of a particular period from a particular geographic area? One of the articulated uses of the Conspectus was posited to be that it would assist the interlibrary loan services. How can it do this? The interlibrary loan user seeks a specific, known item. I know of no documentation proving that the item is more likely to be found at an institution with a high Conspectus number than one with a low Conspectus number it is the luck of the draw, really. Some have posited the use of the Conspectus as a means to allow agreement on distributed collection responsibilities. In a few local cases—most notably the arrangement between Stanford and the University of California, Berkeley—this has been able to work. I am skeptical that it can become a widely-based arrangement. But that is a topic for another day.

I think I owe it to you to try to explain what I think we need to do. If we want a tool to compare collections then we must develop a tool for analysis that more closely reveals the kinds of choices that govern collection development in music. Starting perhaps with each genre, we must be able to articulate the kind of population that we serve as it influences our choice of editions. An institution that grants performance degrees will select rather differently from one that does not. Further, we need a mechanism that will allow us to articulate strengths in particular periods and geographical areas. I do believe that such a schema could be developed.

I do not believe that the Conspectus is that tool. I will ask whether we want to spend the time doing this?

I do not think that collection building is a science. It is an art. No two collections will ever be identical, nor should they be. Each collection is built to serve a particular institution and its users. Each collection reflects an element of chance; gifts, items happened upon by a selector and not bought by others, items requested by users. Each of these elements adds to a collection's strengths. None of this is reflected by the numbers in the Conspectus. Perhaps the distinction is that I see collection development as a microcosm—an entity built up piece by piece—and the Conspectus represents a macrocosm to me. It is something like the difference between the species and the genus. Describing what a collection contains and how it is growing requires a more narrative approach than the one taken by the Conspectus. Comparing collections will, in the long run, be facilitated by the national databases. As more and more libraries convert the catalogs of their collections into machine-readable form we should be able to find machine techniques to analyze and compare them. Meanwhile, those who wish to describe or compare collections must find a more descriptive tool than the RLG Conspectus to use.

Note and Reference

1. The Associated Music Library Group (AMLG) has received funding from the U.S. Department of Education to support a multi-institutional retrospective conversion project. The participating libraries include the Eastman School of Music of the University of Rochester, Indiana University, the University of California at Berkeley, Stanford, Harvard, Yale, and Cornell.

2. Jeffry Larson. "The RLG French Literature Collection Assessment Project. *Collection Management* 6 (1984): 97–114.

APPENDIX

The RLG Music Conspectus Lines*

ID	LC Class	Subjects
MUS1	M1	Collections
MUS2	M1.A1-.A5	American music pre-1860
MUS3	M2	Collections of musical scores
MUS4	M3–3.1	Collected works of individual composers
MUS5	M3.3	First editions
MUS6	M5	Collections of instrumental music
MUS7	M6–19	Organ music
MUS8	M20–39	Piano music
MUS9	M40–175	Music for other solo instruments
MUS10	M176	Instrumental music for motion pictures, radio, television
MUS11	M177–179	Collections of music for two or more solo instruments
MUS12	M180–195	Duets: organ/harmonium
MUS13	M200–216	Piano for three, four, five, etc. hands, two pianos
MUS14	M217–285	Piano and one other instrument
MUS15	M286–298	Duets without keyboard instruments
MUS16	M300–986	Chamber ensembles: trios-nonets and larger combinations
MUS17	M300–986	Chamber music for early instruments
MUS18	M1000–1075	Orchestral music: symphonies, concertos, etc.
MUS19	M1100–1160	String orchestra music: symphonies, concertos
MUS20	M1200–1270	Band music
MUS21	M1350–1366	Music for special ensembles (reduced orch., dance orch., jazz)

MUS22	M1375–1420	Instrumental music for children
MUS23	M1450	Dance music
MUS24	M1470–1480	Chance compositions, electronic music, etc.
MUS25	M1490	Music before 1700
MUS26	M1470–1497	Collections of vocal music: general and ecular
MUS27	M1500–1526	Operas, incidental music, ballets
MUS28	M1527	Vocal music for radio, motion pictures, television
MUS29	M1528–1529	Duets, trios, etc. for solo voices
MUS30	M1530–1546	Choruses with orchestra or other ensemble
MUS31	M1547–1610	Choruses, part-songs
MUS32	M1611–1626	Songs, solo cantatas, recitations
MUS33	M1627	National music: international collection
MUS34	M1628–1677	National music: United States
MUS35	M1678–1685	National music: North America
MUS36	M1686–1694	National music: South America
MUS37	M1687–1789	National music: Europe
MUS38	M1795–1825	National music: Asia
MUS39	M1828	National music: Middle East
MUS40	M1830–1838	National music: Africa
MUS41	M1840–1844	National music: Australia, New Zealand, Pacific Islands
MUS42	M1850–1853	National music: Jewish
MUS43	M1900–1998	Songs of special character, musical games, secular music for children
MUS44	M1999	Collections of sacred vocal music
MUS45	M2000–2007	Oratorios
MUS46	M2010–2017	Services (cyclical choral): Roman Catholic, Protestant, Jewish, etc.
MUS47	M2018–2019	Sacred duets, trios etc. for solo voices
MUS48	M2020–2036	Sacred choruses with orchestra or other ensemble

MUS49	M2060–2101	Sacred choruses, part-songs
MUS50	M2102–2114	Sacred songs, solo cantatas, recitations, etc.
MUS51	M2115–2146	Hymnals
MUS52	M2147–2160	Liturgy and ritual: Roman Catholic, Orthodox
MUS53	M2161–2184	Liturgy and ritual: Protestant, other Christian churches
MUS54	M2186–2188	Liturgy and ritual: Jewish, other non-Christian religions
MUS55	M2190–2196	Sacred vocal music for children
MUS56	M2198–2199	Gospel, revival, temperance, etc.
MUS57	M5000	Unidentified compositions
MUS58	ML1	Periodicals, United States
MUS59	ML4	Periodicals, before 1800
MUS60	ML5	Periodicals, after 1800, foreign
MUS61	ML12–21	Directories
MUS62	ML25–28	Publications of societies
MUS63	ML29–31	Music foundations
MUS64	M32–38	Publications of institutions and festivals
MUS65	ML40–46	Programs and advertisements, scrapbooks
MUS66	ML47–54	Librettos
MUS67	ML55–60	Collected literary works (essays, etc.)
MUS68	ML62–85	Special topics
MUS69	ML86–89	Musical iconography
MUS70	ML90	Writings of musicians
MUS71	ML93–96	Musical paleography
MUS72	ML96.4–96.5	Facsimiles
MUS73	ML97	Catalogs of collectors, dealers, etc.
MUS74	ML100–109	Dictionaries, encyclopedias
MUS75	ML111–134	Music bibliography
MUS76	ML135–155	Catalogs

MUS77	ML156-158	Discography
MUS78	ML159	History before 1800
MUS79	ML160-161	History after 1800
MUS80	ML162-169	Antiquity, history and criticism
MUS81	ML170-190	Medieval and renaissance music, history and criticism
MUS82	ML193	General works
MUS83	ML194	Seventeenth century music, history and criticism
MUS84	ML195	Eighteenth century music, history and criticism
MUS85	ML196	Nineteenth century music, history and criticism
MUS86	ML197	Twentieth century music, history and criticism
MUS87	ML198-239	America: History and criticism (includes Canada, Latin America)
MUS88	ML240-325	Europe, history and criticism
MUS89	ML330-345	Asia, history and criticism
MUS90	ML350	Africa, history and criticism
MUS91	ML360	Australia
MUS92	ML385-429	Biographies
MUS93	ML430-455	Composition
MUS94	ML457	Conducting
MUS95	ML459	Periodicals. Societies. Serials
MUS96	ML460-1092	Musical instruments
MUS97	ML1100-1165	Chamber music
MUS98	ML1200-1270	Orchestral music
MUS99	ML1300-1354	Band music
MUS100	ML1400-1460	Vocal music
MUS101	ML1500-1554	Choral music
MUS102	ML1600-2881	Secular vocal music
MUS103	ML2900-3275	Sacred vocal music
MUS104	ML3300-3354	Program music

MUS105	ML3400–3465	Dance music
MUS106	ML3469–3537	Popular music
MUS107	ML3545	National music (general)
MUS108	ML3549	America (general)
MUS109	ML3550–3563	United States and Canada
MUS110	ML3565	Latin America
MUS111	ML3580–3730	Europe
MUS112	ML3740–3758	Asia
MUS113	ML3760	Africa
MUS114	ML3770–3775	Oceania, Australia
MUS115	ML3776	Jewish music
MUS116	ML3780	Trade, labor, sea, hunting songs
MUS117	ML3785	Music journalism
MUS118	ML3790	Musical industry
MUS119	ML3795	Musical life
MUS120	ML3797	Musicology
MUS121	ML3798–3799	Ethnomusicology
MUS122	ML3800–3923	Philosophy and physics of music
MUS123	ML3930	Literature on music for children
MUS124	MT1	Theory of musical instruction and study
MUS125	MT2–5	History and criticism
MUS126	MT6–18	Music theory
MUS127	MT20–34	Special methods of instruction and study
MUS128	MT35–38	Notation, diction, ear training
MUS129	MT40–67	Composition
MUS130	MT68	Improvisation
MUS131	MT70–84	Orchestration
MUS132	MT86–89	Conducting and organizations
MUS133	MT90–165	Hermenutics
MUS134	MT170–810	Instruments techniques
MUS135	MT820–893	Singing and voice culture

MUS136	MT898–949	Techniques for children
MUS137	MT950	Music to accompany instruction in ballet, etc.
MUS138	MT955–956	Production of operas
MUS139	MT960	Music in theaters

Sound Recordings

ID	LC Class	Subjects
MUS140		Standard concert repertory
MUS141		Film music
MUS142		Musical comedies, revues, etc.
MUS143		Post-1945 Western art music
MUS144		Jazz, reduced orchestra, etc.
MUS145		Popular music (Western commercial music)
MUS146		Pedagogical music
MUS147		Band music
(World Music)		
MUS148		Native American
MUS149		United States & Canada (except Native America)
MUS150		Caribbean
MUS151		Central America & Mexico
MUS152		South America
MUS153		Western Europe
MUS154		Eastern Europe
MUS155		Moslem Africa & the Middle East
MUS156		Black Africa
MUS157		Central & South Asia (India, Afghanistan & Pakistan)
MUS158		East Asia (China, Japan, Korea, Tibet, Mongolia)

MUS159	Southeast Asia (Burma, Thailand, Laos, Vietnam)
MUS160	Indonesia, Philippines, Borneo, Malaysia
MUS161	Australia & Oceania

Bibliography

The following is a selected list of sources on Collection Assessment:

BOOKS, MANUALS, AND GUIDES

American Library Assn., Resources and Technical Services Division, Collection Development Committee. *Guidelines Collection Development.* Ed. by David L. Perkins, 1979.

Association of Research Libraries. Office of Management Studies. *User Survey and the Evaluation of Library Services.* SPEC Kit no. 71. Washington, D.C.: Office of Management Studies, Association of Research Libraries, 1981; *Collection Description and Assessment in ARL Libraries* SPEC Kits: no. 87. Washington, D.C.: Office of Management Studies, Association of Research Libraries, 1982; *Quantitative Collection Analysis: The Conspectus Methodology* SPEC Kits: no.151. Washington, D.C.: Office of Management Studies, Association of Research Libraries, 1989.

Baker, Sharon and F.W. Lancaster. *The Measurement and Evaluation of Library Services.* 2d ed. Arlington, VA: Information Resources Press, 1991.

Gardner, Richard K. *Library Collections: Their Origin, Selection, and Development.* New York: McGraw-Hill, 1981.

Hall, Blaine H. *Collection Assessment Manual for College and University Libraries.* Phoenix, AZ: Oryx, 1985.

Lockett, Barbara, ed. *Guide to the Evaluation of Library Collections.* Chicago: American Library Association, 1989.

Magrill, Rose Mary and John Corbin. *Acquisitions Management and Collection Development in Libraries.* Chicago: American Library Association, 1989.

METRO Collection Inventory Project Manual. New York: METRO, 1991.

Pacific Northwest Collection Assessment Manual. Portland, OR: Fred Meyer Charitable Trust, Library and Information Resources for the Northwest, 1986.

Reed-Scott, Jutta. *Manual for the North American Inventory of Research Library Collections.* Washington, D.C.: Association of Research Libraries, 1988.

MUSIC SPECIFIC STUDIES

Kunselman, Joan D., Peggy Daub and Marion Taylor. "Toward Describing and Assessing the National Music Collection." *Notes* Vol. 43, no. 1 (Sept 1986): 7 - 13.

METRO Music Task Force. *Supplemental Guidelines for Music.* Compiled by Elizabeth Davis, Jane Gottlieb, Honora Raphael, and Kent Underwood. New York: METRO, 1991.

SELECTED ARTICLES AND OTHER STUDIES

Ferguson, Anthony W., Joan Grant and Joel Rutstein. "Internal Uses of the RLG Conspectus." *Journal of Library Administration* 8 (1987): 35–40.

——"The RLG Conspectus: Its Uses and Benefits." *College and Research Libraries* 49 (1988): 197–206.

Futas, Elizabeth and Sheila S. Inter, eds. "Collection Evaluation." *Library Trends* 22 (Winter 1985).

Grover, Mark L. "Collection Assessment in the 1980s." *Collection Building* 8 (1988): 23–26.

Oberg, Larry R. "Evaluating the Conspectus Approach for Smaller Library Collections." *College & Research Libraries* 49 (1988): 187–96.

Stielow, Frederick J. and Helen R. Tibbo. "Collection Analysis in Modern Librarianship: A Stratified Multidimensional Model." *Collection Management* 11, no. 3/4 (1989): 73–91.

Weimers, Eugene, et al. "Collection Evaluation: A Practical Guide to the Literature." *Library Acquisitions: Practice & Theory* 8 (1984): 65–76.

White, Howard D. "Evaluating Subject Collections." In *Annual Review of OCLC Research July 1987-June 1988*: 46–48. Dublin, OH: OCLC Online Computer Library Center, Inc., 1988.

Index

Music Library Association Technical Reports Series

Edited by H. Stephen Wright

18. *Careers in Music Librarianship: Perspectives From the Field* compiled by Carol Tatian, 1991.
19. *In Celebration of Revised 780: Music in the Dewey Decimal Classification, Edition 20* compiled by Richard B. Wursten, 1990.
20. *Space Utilization in Music Libraries* compiled by James P. Cassaro, 1992.
21. *Archival Information Processing for Sound Recordings: The Design of a Database for the Rodgers and Hammerstein Archives of Recorded Sound* by David Thomas, 1992.
22. *Collection Assessment in Music Libraries* edited by Jane Gottlieb, 1994.
23. *Knowing the Score: Preserving Collections of Music* compiled by Mark Roosa and Jane Gottlieb, 1994.
24. *World Music in Music Libraries* edited by Carl Rahkonen, 1994.
25. *Cataloging Musical Moving Image Material: A Guide to the Bibliographic Control of Videorecordings and Films of Musical Performances and Other Music-Related Moving Image Material: With Examples in MARC Format* edited by Lowell Ashley, 1996
26. *Guide to Writing Collection Development Policies for Music,* by Amanda Maple and Jean Morrow, 2001.
27. *Music Librarianship at the Turn of the Century,* edited by Richard Griscom, assistant editor Amanda Maple, 2000.
28. *Cataloging Sheet Music: Guidelines for Use with AACR2 and the MARC format,* compiled and edited by Lois Schultz and Sarah Shaw, 2003.